W9-BXZ-878

SOLID
FOOL'S
GOLD

SOLID FOOL'S GOLD

DETOURS ON THE WAY TO CONVENTIONAL WISDOM

by Bill James

SOLID FOOL'S GOLD
Detours on the Way to Conventional Wisdom
by Bill James

Edited by Gregory F. Augustine Pierce
Cover design by Tom A. Wright
Text design and typesetting by Patricia Lynch

Copyright © 2011 by Bill James

Published by ACTA Sports, a division of ACTA Publications,
4848 N. Clark Street, Chicago, IL 60077 (800) 397-2282
www.actapublications.com

All rights reserved. No part of this publication may be reproduced or transmitted in any form or by any means, electronic or mechanical, including photocopying and recording, or by any information and retrieval system, including the Internet, without permission from the publisher. Permission is hereby given to use short excerpts (under 500 words) with proper citation in reviews and marketing copy, online blogs, and scholarly papers and class handouts.

Library of Congress Number: 2011923351
ISBN: 978-0-87946-459-2
Printed in the United States of America by McNaughton & Gunn, Inc.
Year: 20 19 18 17 16 15 14 13 12 11
Printing: 10 9 8 7 6 5 4 3 2 First

Contents

INTRODUCTION

———•———

Hi; this is Bill James. Throughout the course of every year I write a lot of articles which are published on Bill James Online (Billjamesonline.com). These articles are not read by very many people, because, frankly, mostly they're not worth reading. No, seriously; I don't know whether they're worth reading or not; that's the reader's decision, not the writer's. The reason they are not read by very many people is that we charge $3 a month for access to the online, and we're not all that good at marketing the site, so...not an awful lot of people read them.

A few of these articles, however, may be worth publishing on actual chopped-up-and-bleached trees. I said *may be*; again, this is not my decision. That would be a publisher's decision.

Greg Pierce is a publisher; specifically, he's the head of ACTA Publications in Chicago. Evanston? Not sure; I know you can walk to Wrigley from there. Must be Chicago.

Anyway, Greg and I have worked together for several years. Greg, for reasons known only to himself and possibly his priest, chooses to read all of that stuff that I publish online, with the idea of finding any parts of it that might be worth publishing in a form such as that you hold in your hand. This, then, is a collection of articles that have been previously published—barely. Published, but not widely read. The only article in here that has been widely read is an article that is being re-published from the *1983 Baseball Abstract*; that was widely read in its time, but we thought perhaps you might enjoy seeing it again, in the same way that you might enjoy seeing *Terms of Endearment* again, or *Risky Business*, or *Gorky Park*, or *War Games*, or *Stray Dogs*. Those were all movies that came out in 1983. So was *Yentl*; but absolutely nobody wants to see Yentl again. It's been 28 years; I have almost completely forgiven my wife for making me see it the first time. Where was I?

Oh, yes...Greg Pierce reads through the hundreds of pages of stuff that I publish annually on Bill James Online, and finds articles that might deserve to be enshrined in paper. Some of these articles could be considered serious baseball research, to the extent that research about baseball can be considered a serious undertaking. Some of them are not. Some of them have nothing to do with baseball. Some of them have to do with tipping your pizza delivery guy, or with Olympic NASCAR racing. You will not forget, while reading this book, that I am essentially a baseball writer, but perhaps you will occasionally allow me to stray off the subject.

I will not do anything here to help you win your fantasy league because, frankly, I don't care whether you win your fantasy league or not; it's not my problem.

We hope you enjoy our book; we have tried to find articles that are fun to read and stimulating to think about, and we have tried not to waste your time with stuff that is only useful to you if you are wondering whether you should draft Kevin Kouzmanoff in the fifth round or wait to the sixth. We hope you like the book, and if you do we will publish some additional collections a little bit like it, but if you don't and the Cubs meet the Red Sox in the World Series, we will consider it a good year anyway. Thanks for reading.

—·—

Predicting RBI

by Bill James

A couple of years ago, I went looking for a formula that would predict RBI based on a player's other hitting stats, and I found a really good one. It's Total Bases divided by four, plus Home Runs. That's all you have to do; divide a player's Total Bases by four, add his Home Runs; that's about how many runs he will drive in.

Reviewing the 2010 season for this data...the following hitters matched or almost matched their expected RBI:

Hitter	Team	RBI	Expected RBI
Braun,Ryan	Brewers	103	103
Wright,David	Mets	103	103
Tulowitzki,Troy	Rockies	95	94
Hunter,Torii	Angels	90	90
Reynolds,Mark	Diamondbacks	85	86
Kouzmanoff,Kevin	Athletics	71	71
Ludwick,Ryan	Padres	69	68
Gutierrez,Franklin	Mariners	64	64
Burrell,Pat	Giants	64	64
Stewart,Ian	Rockies	61	61
Span,Denard	Twins	58	58
Olivo,Miguel	Rockies	58	58
Pierzynski,A.J.	White Sox	56	55

Hitter	Team	RBI	Expected RBI
Cantu,Jorge	Rangers	56	57
Cust,Jack	Athletics	52	51
Johnson,Chris	Astros	52	52
Kearns,Austin	Yankees	49	50
Rollins,Jimmy	Phillies	41	41
Valencia,Danny	Twins	40	41
Maier,Mitch	Royals	39	40
Torrealba,Yorvit	Padres	37	38
Duncan,Shelley	Indians	36	35
Hairston,Scott	Padres	36	36
Molina,Bengie	Rangers	36	36
Valdez,Wilson	Phillies	35	34
Nady,Xavier	Cubs	33	34
Kennedy,Adam	Nationals	31	31
Diaz,Matt	Braves	31	32
Avila,Alex	Tigers	31	32
Vizquel,Omar	White Sox	30	31
Bradley,Milton	Mariners	29	29
Young,Delwyn	Pirates	28	27
Iannetta,Chris	Rockies	27	27
Sweeney,Mike	Phillies	26	25
Lowell,Mike	Red Sox	26	25
Lucroy,Jonathan	Brewers	26	27
Janish,Paul	Reds	25	24
Church,Ryan	Diamondbacks	25	24
Laird,Gerald	Tigers	25	26
Ka'aihue,Kila	Royals	25	26
Moreland,Mitch	Rangers	25	26
Teahen,Mark	White Sox	25	26

Of the 427 major league hitters who drove in ten or more runs in 2010, 166 came within three RBI of matching their expectation. On the other hand, the following players drove in significantly more runs than expected:

Name	Team	RBI	Expected RBI	Difference
Rodriguez,Alex	Yankees	125	96	+29
Young,Delmon	Twins	112	91	+21
Loney,James	Dodgers	88	68	+20
Zobrist,Ben	Rays	75	58	+17
Molina,Yadier	Cardinals	62	46	+16
Kubel,Jason	Twins	92	76	+16
Cervelli,Francisco	Yankees	38	22	+16

While the following wazarongs drove in less:

Name	Team	RBI	Expected RBI	Difference
Suzuki,Ichiro	Mariners	43	73	-30
Johnson,Kelly	Diamondbacks	71	99	-28
Phillips,Brandon	Reds	59	85	-26
Jackson,Austin	Tigers	41	66	-25
McCutchen,Andrew	Pirates	56	80	-24
Weeks,Rickie	Brewers	83	105	-22
Markakis,Nick	Orioles	60	81	-21
Aybar,Erick	Angels	29	49	-20
Aviles,Mike	Royals	32	52	-20
Wells,Vernon	Blue Jays	88	107	-19
Edmonds,Jim	Reds	23	42	-19
Drew,Stephen	Diamondbacks	61	80	-19
Theriot,Ryan	Dodgers	29	48	-19
Bautista,Jose	Blue Jays	124	142	-18
Bruce,Jay	Reds	70	88	-18
Prado,Martin	Braves	66	84	-18
Reyes,Jose	Mets	54	71	-17
Fielder,Prince	Brewers	83	100	-17
Snider,Travis	Blue Jays	32	49	-17
Scutaro,Marco	Red Sox	56	72	-16
Lewis,Fred	Blue Jays	36	52	-16
Morgan,Nyjer	Nationals	24	40	-16
Werth,Jayson	Phillies	85	101	-16

Research has shown that, when a player drives in more runs than expected, this is on average about 50% because he had a higher-than-expected number of RBI opportunities, and about 50% because he hit well with runners on base and with runners in scoring position. Alex Emmanuel Rodriguez, for example, had a .774 OPS with the bases empty, but .924 with men on base. This creates more than an expected number of RBI, and his number of chances was also a little high. Delmon Young hit .355 with runners in scoring position, and was also fourth in the league in at bats with runners in scoring position.

———

AND IN A RELATED STORY

by Bill James

On January 11, 2010, Mark McGwire acknowledged in multiple venues that he had, in fact, used steroids and Human Growth Hormone. McGwire issued a statement, gave an interview to Bob Costas, answered questions from reporters in a phone conference, and made numerous other personal phone calls to apologize and accept responsibility for misleading people about the issue. Reaction to his apology was almost universally negative.

And in a related story, former New York Yankee outfielder Roger Maris has apologized in a televised interview, broadcast early Wednesday morning on HVEN TV, for using eight extra games and expansion pitching to break the single-season home run record of previous record holder Babe Ruth. Maris was interviewed by the sainted sportscaster Curt Gowdy in a studio just two miles inside the pearly gates late Tuesday afternoon.

Maris, breaking into tears numerous times throughout the interview, acknowledged that he did in fact play 161 games in 1961, as many observers had insisted for years that he must have, and also that he did hit some home runs against pitchers who might not have been in the league were it not for expansion.

"It was the worst thing I have ever done, and I am so ashamed," Maris sobbed.

Asked by Gowdy why it has taken him 48 years to apologize, Maris said he was acting on the advice of his attorneys, and also expressed a desire to protect his family. "I didn't feel it was wrong at the time," Maris said. "Everybody else was using the eight extra games. Why shouldn't I?"

Maris' belated apology was immediately denounced by several snarky commentators, who felt that Maris must be insincere, since

Maris suggested that he could have broken the record without the eight extra games and the expansion pitchers.

"Sure I could have," Maris said. "If you'll look, you'll see that I didn't hit ANY home runs in 1961 in the first ten games of the season, so actually I hit the 61 homers in just 151 games. The last 151."

"Everybody else in the league was hitting home runs off of Pete Burnside," Maris said. "I figured, why shouldn't I? If any young hitter ever asked me about it, I would plead with them not to hit any home runs off of Pete Burnside or Ed Palmquist. It's just not worth it, what it does to your soul."

Maris also announced that he had called the widow of the late Babe Ruth, and apologized to her as well for outperforming the Bambino.

"What did she say to you?" Gowdy asked.

"She asked if I could send along some Budweiser with the apology," Maris responded.

"She still regards her husband as the legitimate home run record holder," Gowdy remarked.

"She has every right to," Maris responded.

Maris' agent had requested that Howard Cosell do the interview, but Cosell could not be located, and it is suspected that he may be working for HVEN's arch-rival HLL, the hottest network on the air.

And in another related story, Babe Ruth has requested an interview, in which it is rumored that he will acknowledge using a corked bat for most of his career, taking advantage of outrageous favoritism from the umpires, and being an unworthy role model for America's youth due to his widely reported drinking and whoring. That interview is being delayed while Ruth tries to figure out who held the home run record before he did, as he needs to call somebody's widow or children and apologize in vague, unintelligible terms. Among the candidates for Ruth's apology are the widows and descendants of Gavy Cravath, Buck Freeman, Roger Connor and Ned Williamson. If you know where any of these people can be located, please call 1-800-RAPTURE or contact Rick Warren personally with details.

———·—·—

Random vs Responsive Performance by Starting Pitchers

by Bill James

I. The Sins of My Youth

One of the central questions of sabermetrics, stated in the in obscure, unemotional language favored by academics and bankers testifying before Congress, is to what extent player performance is responsive to conditions, and to what extent it occurs in random patterns. This dispute has hundreds of manifestations.

The experts and analysts of my youth universally believed that player performance was responsive to conditions. They believed that there were large-scale, omnipresent interactions between situations and performance. They believed that some hitters hit much better in clutch situations than at other times, while others fell short in the same conditions. They believed that some hitters were RBI men, meaning that they had the ability to hit better in RBI situations. They believed that if a base stealer reached base, the next hitter would hit better because the pitcher's attention was divided. They believed that a power hitter would hit better if he had another good hitter behind him, to protect him. If one team hit .240 and scored 750 runs while another hit .270 and scored 700 runs, they attributed this to timely performance and to subtle, unmeasured skills like hitting behind the runner and going from first to third on a single. They believed that good teams won the close games because they executed when the game was on the line. They believed that great players dominated in the heat of a pennant race. If one pitcher went 18-11 with an ERA of 4.00 while a teammate went 9-15 with an ERA of 3.60, they believed absolutely and without question that this happened because the 18-11 pitcher had pitched better when the game was on the line.

They believed these things, and they were the experts, and so, in 1975, *I* believed these things. I had been told all of my life that these things were true, and I accepted that they were. When I began to study the game in a systematic way, I expected to find obvious and abundant evidence of these responsive performance interactions.

I couldn't find them.

I couldn't find *any* of them, basically. I couldn't find (nor could other researchers) any evidence that certain players had an ability to hit in the clutch, nor an ability to hit in RBI situations. I couldn't find that when a base stealer reached base, the next hitter hit better, because in fact he doesn't. I couldn't find that any hitter hit meaningfully better with "protection" behind him, because in fact nobody does.

I *did* come to understand why one team would hit .240 and score 750 runs, while another would hit .270 but score 700 runs, but the explanation, nine times in ten, *wasn't* clutch hitting or subtle skills; it was that the team that hit .240 had more power and more walks. With regard to good teams and close games, I found that the opposite of the conventional wisdom was true and that good teams *don't* in fact win the close games and that .600 teams are .550 teams in one-run games.

And I did come to understand why one pitcher would go 18-11 with a 4.00 ERA, while a teammate would go 9-15 with a 3.60 ERA. It was offensive support. It was *entirely* offensive support, I argued. There was no evidence—or so I thought at the time—that it had anything at all to do with pitching well when the game was close, or, indeed, that there was any such ability.

I was widely attacked for saying these things, which was one of the best things that ever happened to me. The attacks were of two natures: 1) That I was ignorant for knowing nothing about the small skills and subtleties of the game which could not be measured by mere numbers, and 2) That by arguing that player's performance did not change with game situations, I was arguing against character and courage. Players came through in the clutch, people chose to believe, because they were Men of Character. By arguing that there was no evidence of any such ability, I was seen to be arguing against the relevance of character.

Conventional wisdom in these areas is not what it once was. What the experts and analysts of 40 years ago believed, a certain number of them still believe today, and that "certain number" is near 100% of the on-air experts. Still, the situation is very different than it was, because everybody now has data. Everybody now has batting averages with runners in scoring position, and run support numbers for pitchers, and other points of data that grind away daily at the misconceptions that loomed as monsters in days of yore. It is different because everybody has data, and it is different as well because there is now another community of analysts and experts, a community whose expertise is based not merely on playing the game, but on actually studying it.

II. Some Doubts

There are, of course, some documented interactions between situations and performances. It is not that these responsive performance variations don't exist, but that many of them don't exist at all, while those that do either are of much less significance than was once believed or act in the opposite manner from what was long assumed.

Among the heretical denunciations of my youth, however, the one with which I am least comfortable is the belief that pitchers have zero ability to pitch to the level of the game—that is, in the example above, that ALL of the difference between the 18-11 pitcher and the 9-15 pitcher is in offensive support, and that none of it is explained by the 18-11 pitcher pitching to the level that was required to win the game.

Pitching is different from hitting in this respect: pitching is planned, whereas hitting is reacting. A hitter who tried to "bear down" at key moments of the game would almost certainly perform worse, not better, as he would just be putting a lot of tension in his swing, disrupting his normal mechanical actions. A pitcher, on the other hand, reasonably *could* maximize his outcomes by "bearing down" at key moments of the game. A pitcher could "set up" hitters by throwing secondary pitches with the bases empty, but using his best stuff when the game was on the line. A pitcher can coast when the game is out of hand, just working his way calmly through the innings without worrying too much about runs scoring. I'm not saying this is *true*, but it's easier to visualize it working for a pitcher than for a hitter.

One of the arguments I made, thirty years ago, was this: that if you took the "A" and "B" parts of that set—the 18-11 pitcher being the "A" part—if you took the A and B parts of those sets and projected them forward, the "B" pitchers would perform better in subsequent seasons—not only better in terms of ERA, but better in terms of wins and losses as well. There was no evidence of a carryover effect here, thus no evidence of a real skill.

There were other arguments that I made, as well, but the problem with *that* argument is this: if *every* pitcher pitched to the level of the contest, and did so regularly and on a large scale, then of course we could easily identify that effect, and demonstrate that it was true. But what if just one pitcher in all of baseball had this skill?

If just one pitcher had this trait, the aggregate data would look the same as if no pitcher had this trait. But what if 15 or 20% of pitchers had this trait, and what if the trait itself was fairly small and difficult to document? Would I have been able, under those circumstances, to recognize the differences between a universe of pitchers, *none* of whom had this trait, and a universe of pitchers, 15 or 20% of the total, who had this trait to some small degree?

Frankly I could not have. I am not well trained in statistical methods. I think by analogy and work by intuition, with a sort of bumper-sticker understanding of scientific methods. It seems to me that if only a minority of pitchers had this trait, and if the trait was of relatively modest scale in those cases, that I would almost certainly have missed it.

Well, is it reasonable to think that only 15 to 20% of pitchers would have a certain trait?

Sure it is.

What percentage of pitchers can throw an effective change-up? What percentage of pitchers can throw 95? What percentage of pitchers can throw left-handed? What percentage of pitchers have a four-pitch mix? What percentage of pitchers can pick a runner off first base?

Some pitchers have traits that other pitchers do not have. It is not inherently unreasonable to think that some pitchers would have this particular, let's call it "clutch", trait and others would not, any more than it is unreasonable to think that some outfielders would be able to throw well enough to play right field and others would not.

I'm not apologizing; I did honest work and reported on it honestly. I am simply saying that, looking back at it from a distance of time, I find my own argument to be not entirely convincing.

III. The Curious Case of Mike Morgan

Recently, as Livan Hernandez moved past 2800 innings in his career, I veered into a discussion with the subscribers of Bill James Online based on whether he might be the worst pitcher ever to have such a long career. In the course of this discussion Mike Morgan and his career 141-186 won-lost record were mentioned, probably by me. It was pointed out to me in response that, while Morgan's won-lost record was 45 games under water, Morgan was only 36 runs worse than an average pitcher—park and league adjusted—and thus, his won-lost record was basically attributable to the teams that he pitched for.

Or was it?

Actually, the teams that Mike Morgan pitched for weren't all that bad. Morgan pitched for 25 teams in his career. Not counting Morgan's decisions, 12 of those teams had losing records, 12 of them had winning records, and the other was exactly .500. The career winning percentage of Mike Morgan's teams other than when Mike Morgan was pitching, weighted by Morgan's number of decisions each year, was .494. Had Morgan had the same winning percentage as the rest of his team in every season and the same number of decisions that he actually had, his career won-lost record would have been 162-165. Which, by the way, would have made him Bump Hadley. Bump Hadley, most famous as the pitcher who skulled Mickey Cochrane, had a career record of 161-165, with a 4.24 ERA.

Might it not be true that Morgan's runs allowed rate was misleading because Morgan failed to pitch well when he had a chance to win the game?

In fact, it is true. Morgan did not pitch well when he had a chance to win, and his won-lost record does reflect his failure to do so.

I will document that this is true by comparing Morgan with John Burkett, and edge us toward a method to make the appropriate adjustments based on that.

IV. MORGAN AND BURKETT

We are dealing here with the issue of whether some pitchers may have an ability to pitch especially well when they have an opportunity to win the game. Let us contrast Mike Morgan with John Burkett. Morgan made 411 starts in his career; Burkett made 423. Morgan had a career ERA of 4.23; Burkett, of 4.31. Morgan allowed 4.65 runs per nine innings, earned and un-earned; Burkett allowed 4.67. Morgan pitched from 1978 to 2002: Burkett, from 1987 to 2003. The two were teammates with the Rangers in 1999.

Yet while Morgan was 45 games *under* .500 in his career, Burkett—with essentially the same numbers, in the same era—was 30 games *over* .500. Yes, offensive support did have a good deal to do with that. Burkett *did* pitch for better teams. Had Burkett had the same won-lost record as the rest of his team in every season, his career record would have been 159-143, whereas Morgan, as I said, would have been 162-165.

But Burkett also pitched better when he needed to pitch better to get a win.

John Burkett was shut out 20 times in his career, and his personal won-lost record in those games was 0-19; Morgan was shut out 28 times, and his personal won-lost record in those games was 0-27.

Morgan took a bigger hit, yes, but the two pitchers' winning percentages, when they were shut out, were the same:

Working with 0 runs		
Morgan	0-27	.000
Burkett	0-19	.000

Of course, *all* pitchers have a .000 winning percentage when they are shut out, it being impossible to win those games.

Morgan also had more games in his career in which he was limited to one run, 42 to 33. But you *can* win a game with one run, if you pitch well enough, and Burkett did this more times in his career than did Morgan:

Working with 1 run		
Burkett	3-25	.107
Morgan	2-35	.054

Advantage, Burkett—a one-game advantage.

Mike Morgan had 65 starts in his career in which his team scored 2 runs; Burkett had 61. Burkett won 13 of those games; Morgan, 3.

Working with 2 runs		
Burkett	13-38	.255
Morgan	3-45	.063

Advantage, Burkett—and this time it's a big one. Given just 2 runs to work with, Burkett rose to the occasion 13 times, Morgan only 3 times. It looks like a ten-game advantage for Burkett, although it's actually less than that.

Working with 3 runs		
Morgan	21-34	.382
Burkett	15-28	.349

Advantage, Morgan—a one- or two-game edge. But working with four runs:

Working with 4 runs		
Burkett	18-11	.621
Morgan	20-19	.513

Advantage, Burkett—another three games or thereabout. Working with five runs:

Working with 5 runs		
Burkett	20-4	.833
Morgan	20-10	.667

Advantage, Burkett. Working with six runs:

Working with 6 runs		
Burkett	18-4	.818
Morgan	16-4	.800

Advantage, Burkett. Morgan does have a one- or two-game advantage when working with seven runs:

Working with 7 runs		
Morgan	10-1	.909
Burkett	17-4	.810

But when working with eight or more, Burkett is back ahead:

Working with 8 runs		
Burkett	59-1	.983
Morgan	35-3	.921

V. Method

Burkett clearly did a better job of rising to the occasion, over his career, than did Morgan, and this clearly had value to his teams. But how do we quantify that value?

Of course, I have examined this issue many times before over the course of the years. I think most recently in something I published about Bert Blyleven and Don Sutton. But while I have studied this issue before, the two new methods that I have to offer here are, I am confident, the best methods I have ever developed to address this issue, this "ability to respond" by a starting pitcher.

Here's what I did. What we're trying to calculate here is the pitcher's "effective runs allowed rate", based on his ability to win the game with a given level of offensive support. (Let's let ERAR standing for "Effective Runs Allowed Rate"; I despise acronyms, but sometimes you've got to do what you've got to do.)

Of course, no pitcher has any ability to win the game when his team is shut out, therefore it's not relevant data to what we're trying to calculate. Therefore we'll set that data aside for right now.

At the other levels of run support, we're going to work not with the pitcher's *individual* won-lost record, but rather, with the won-lost record of his team. I believe that this gives us a better working platform. Suppose that two pitchers both have won-lost records of 16-4 when supported by 7 runs, but that one pitcher's team is 17-5 in those games, while the other pitchers' team is 17-11. The bullpen has lost the game for his team six more times, but are those six extra losses relevant to establishing the performance level of the starting pitcher?

Yes, of course they are. If you leave with the ballgame 7-6, there is a very good chance that your bullpen is going to blow the game for you. If you leave with the ballgame 7-0, there is very little chance that the bullpen is going to give it away. The team performance record, in my view, gives a more thorough look at what has really happened than the individual record.

OK, we'll work with three pitchers here: John Burkett, Mike Morgan and Whitey Ford. When the team scored one run with this pitcher on the mound, John Burkett's teams were 3-30, Mike Morgan's teams were 3-39, and Whitey Ford's teams, within the games documented by Retrosheet, were 10-28 with one tie.

Burkett with 1 run	3-30
Morgan with 1 run	3-39
Whitey Ford with 1 run	10-28

We know how many runs the pitcher's team had to work with in those games, right? It's one run a game. Burkett's teams had 33 runs to work with, Morgan's teams had 39, Ford's teams had 38:

Burkett with 1 run	3-30	33 runs
Morgan with 1 run	3-39	42 runs
Ford with 1 run	10-28	38 runs

Now it's Sabermetrics 101. If Team A scored 33 runs in a set of games and their won-lost record was 3-30, how many runs did they probably allow? Apply the Pythagorean Formula. To get Burkett's "effective runs allowed" we take the losses (30), divided by the wins (3), take the square root of that, multiply by 33 and you get:

Burkett with 1 run	3-30	33 runs	104 runs allowed
Morgan with 1 run	3-39	42 runs	151 runs allowed
Ford with 1 run	10-28	38 runs	64 runs allowed

Divide the runs allowed by the games, and you have the effective runs allowed rate:

Burkett with 1 run	104 runs in 33 games	3.16 runs per game ERAR
Morgan with 1 run	151 runs in 42 games	3.61 runs per game ERAR
Ford with 1 run	64 runs in 38 games	1.67 runs per game ERAR

What I am saying is not that Burkett allowed 3.16 runs 9 innings in these games, but that his teams won with the frequency expected *if* he allowed 3.16 runs per game.

With 2 runs to work with, Burkett's teams were 15-46, which is pretty good, but Ford's teams were 19-22, which is *really* good. Applying the same method, one can calculate the effective runs allowed rate for each pitcher, working with 2 runs:

Burkett with 2 runs	15-46	214 runs in 61 games	3.50 runs per game ERAR
Morgan with 2 runs	9-56	324 runs in 65 games	4.99 runs per game ERAR
Ford with 2 runs	19-22	88 runs in 41 games	2.15 runs per game ERAR

And we can compare them when working with 3 runs:

Burkett with 3 runs	24-37	227 runs in 61 games	3.72 runs per gameERAR
Morgan with 3 runs	27-39	238 runs in 66 games	3.61 runs per gameERAR
Ford with 3 runs	45-30	184 runs in 75 games	2.45 runs per gameERAR

At the level of three runs to work with, as mentioned before, Morgan was better than Burkett, although neither one of them was Whitey Ford.

VI. The Other Method

At this point we could rush ahead to our conclusion, but perhaps it is more fun to stop and admire the data a little bit, make some use of our other method, shake out the problems and challenges of the method, and then work back to our conclusion.

I looked at all starts by all pitchers within the Retrosheet data, 1952 to 2009. Retrosheet, for those of you who don't know, is a volunteer organization run by Dave Smith which collects and publishes accounts of major league baseball games. Using the Retrosheet data, I looked at every pitcher's won-lost record when his team scored no runs, one run, two runs, etc.

Of course, no pitcher won any games in which his team was shut out, but the pitcher who was shut out most often was Nolan Ryan, who was victimized by 66 shutouts in his career. But these games are excluded from the studies of Effective Runs.

Working with one run, the number one pitcher in the data was Dean Chance, 1964 Cy Young Award winner. Chance's teams, in his career, were 17-41 when they scored just one run. The overall winning percentage of teams that scored 1 run, in the Retrosheet data, was .101. Chance's teams were 11 games better than expectation in that situation.

These were the top ten pitchers in modern baseball history in games with just one run to work with:

First	Last	Games	Team W	Team L	Gain	Won	Lost
Dean	Chance	58	17	41	11.1	16	35
Greg	Maddux	84	19	65	10.5	16	61
Nolan	Ryan	104	19	85	8.5	14	75
Sandy	Koufax	33	11	22	7.7	11	19
Gaylord	Perry	86	16	69	7.4	13	64
Bert	Blyleven	85	15	70	6.4	15	65
Chuck	Finley	56	12	44	6.3	10	40
Ferguson	Jenkins	57	12	45	6.2	12	42
Whitey	Ford	39	10	28	6.2	8	27
** Carl	Morton	31	9	22	5.9	7	18

Chance individually was 16-35 in games with just one run to work with; his teams were 17-41. These, on the other hand, were the pitchers with the worst won-lost records while working without a net:

First	Last	Games	Team W	Team L	Gain	Won	Lost
** Steve	Rogers	41	1	46	-3.7	1	44
Jon	Lieber	32	0	32	-3.2	0	25
Bartolo	Colon	31	0	31	-3.1	0	26
Jack	Fisher	40	1	39	-3.0	1	33
Bill	Gullickson	39	1	38	-2.9	1	33
Pete	Falcone	29	0	29	-2.9	0	27
Bill	Wegman	29	0	29	-2.9	0	26
John	Smoltz	38	1	37	-2.8	1	32
Derek	Lowe	28	0	28	-2.8	0	24
John	Thomson	28	0	28	-2.8	0	26

**Carl Morton was the National League rookie of the year in 1970; Steve Rogers could have won the same award for the same team three years later, although he didn't. Rogers certainly had a better career than Morton—but Morton's teams were 9-22 when working with just one run, while Rogers' teams were 1-46. But working with two runs, Rogers was 22-37—a very good record—while Morton was 5-28. Morton beats Rogers by ten games in games with one run; Rogers beats Morton by ten games in games with two runs. The overall winning percentage of all teams with 2 runs to work with was .247, and these were the top ten pitchers in modern baseball history in those games:

First	Last	Games	Team W	Team L	Gain	Won	Lost
Tom	Seaver	91	43	48	20.6	38	38
Randy	Johnson	76	35	41	16.3	30	31
Mike	Cuellar	56	30	26	16.2	27	21
Bob	Gibson	66	31	34	15.0	28	31
Vida	Blue	68	29	39	12.2	26	35
Sandy	Koufax	48	24	24	12.2	20	19
Steve	Carlton	102	37	65	11.8	34	55
Phil	Niekro	103	36	66	10.8	32	57
Al	Downing	55	24	31	10.4	19	21
Claude	Osteen	68	27	41	10.2	21	32

Tom Seaver pitched .500 ball when his teams scored just two runs (38-38), and his teams over-achieved in those games by twenty-plus games. I don't know whether or not that's more amazing than Mike Cuellar. Cuellar was 27-21 in his career when his team scored two runs for him. Now *that's* impressive.

On the other end of that scale was our friend Mike Morgan, whose team lost seven more two-run games than they "should" have:

First	Last	Games	Team W	Team L	Gain	Won	Lost
Mike	Morgan	65	9	56	-7.0	3	45
Jim	Colborn	35	2	33	-6.6	2	27
Tony	Cloninger	30	1	29	-6.4	1	25
Pete	Schourek	31	2	29	-5.6	2	21
Bryn	Smith	39	4	35	-5.6	2	27
Don	Cardwell	44	5	38	-5.6	5	36
Mike	Moore	55	8	47	-5.6	7	41
Eric	Milton	27	1	25	-5.4	1	19
Jesse	Jefferson	29	2	27	-5.2	2	25
Frank	Tanana	100	20	80	-4.7	18	68

Let's start tracking the aggregate performance. Tom Seaver, based on his strong performance in games with two runs, is now in first place:

First	Last	Total 1-2
Tom	Seaver	25.7
Greg	Maddux	20.6
Mike	Cuellar	19.8
Sandy	Koufax	19.8
Nolan	Ryan	18.4
Bob	Gibson	18.1
Steve	Carlton	17.7
Randy	Johnson	17.6
Gaylord	Perry	16.3
Bert	Blyleven	15.8

While Mike Morgan and Livan Hernandez are bringing up the rear:

First	Last	Total 1-2
Mike	Morgan	-8.3
Livan	Hernandez	-7.2
Mike	Moore	-7.1

I'm referencing a different method here, of course. My basic, serious method for analyzing this data is the one I was working with in the last section, but to compile these charts, I'm doing something different. Since the winning percentage of teams that scored two runs in a game was .247, I'm comparing each pitcher to a .247 winning percentage. Tom Seaver, at two runs, was twenty games better than a .247 winning percentage. There are problems with that method, which I will leave you to spot on your own, but it's still useful, and as we will see it produces a list of best pitchers which is pretty solidly identifiable as a list of best pitchers.

Three runs. The number one pitcher, at being able to win the game with three runs, was Seaver's American League contemporary and rival, Jim Palmer:

First	Last	Games	Team W	Team L	Gain	Won	Lost
Jim	Palmer	86	55	31	21.6	47	28
Don	Sutton	116	65	51	19.9	52	33
Bob	Gibson	86	50	36	16.6	44	31
Greg	Maddux	118	62	56	16.2	46	44
Tommy	John	103	56	47	16.0	41	32
Nolan	Ryan	116	61	55	15.9	51	43
Whitey	Ford	75	45	30	15.9	34	18
Sam	McDowell	69	41	28	14.2	30	21
Vida	Blue	80	45	35	13.9	38	29
Tom	Seaver	113	57	56	13.1	51	40

Palmer won almost two-thirds of his games, given three runs to work with, but Seaver is on the good list again, while Sandy Koufax, for a change, is not. The overall winning percentage of starting pitchers working with three runs was .396. But Pat Rapp, given three runs to work with, was 3-21:

First	Last	Games	Team W	Team L	Gain	Won	Lost
Pat	Rapp	33	5	28	-7.8	3	21
Tim	Belcher	46	11	35	-6.9	8	26
Brad	Radke	64	18	46	-6.9	13	32

Seaver is still in first place, Palmer moving up to third:

First	Last	Total 1-3
Tom	Seaver	38.8
Greg	Maddux	36.7
Jim	Palmer	35.2
Bob	Gibson	34.7
Nolan	Ryan	34.3
Whitey	Ford	30.9
Don	Sutton	30.7
Sandy	Koufax	30.6
Vida	Blue	28.2
Gaylord	Perry	28.1

While Pat Rapp has now claimed the bottom of the chart.

First	Last	Total 1-3
Pat	Rapp	-12.8
Paul	Byrd	-11.1
Jim	Abbott	-10.6

Mike Morgan, with a positive performance at the three-run level (27-39), has escaped not merely the last spot, but the bottom 40. Are you rooting for somebody here? You should pick out somebody to root for; it makes the competition more fun. And where's Clemens, by the way? Are he and Mindy in a back closet or something?

These are the overall winning percentages, for teams and starting pitchers, with each level of offensive support:

	Team Winning Percentage	Starting Pitcher Winning Percentage
0 Runs	.000	.000
1 Run	.101	.098
2 Runs	.247	.242
3 Runs	.389	.396
4 Runs	.528	.564
5 Runs	.641	.707
6 Runs	.727	.815
7 Run	.802	.875
8 Runs or More	.907	.957

OK, four runs. At the four-run level, the most effective pitcher at delivering a win for his team was...Roger Clemens:

First	Last	Games	Team W	Team L	Gain	Won	Lost
Roger	Clemens	97	72	25	20.8	56	19
Nolan	Ryan	100	70	30	17.2	55	21
David	Cone	65	48	17	13.7	33	13
Bob	Welch	67	47	20	11.6	36	13
Steve	Carlton	89	58	31	11.0	47	17
Larry	Dierker	38	31	7	10.9	25	7
Dave	McNally	61	43	18	10.8	35	10
Ron	Guidry	56	4	16	10.4	34	11
Warren	Spahn	58	41	17	10.4	37	14
Al	Leiter	64	44	20	10.2	35	10

Clemens' winning percentage, given four runs to work with, was just short of .750, both for him individually and for the team.

In a way, these groups are like "years" of a player's career. We add up what the players did in 1991, in 1992, in 1993, etc. Probably the same pitcher wasn't the #1 guy each year; one year it was Clemens, another year it was Maddux, another year it was The Unit. We add them together to form a picture of the whole. Same here; some guys do great in one group of games, some guys in another. It's a competition.

In first place in the competition, right now, is Nolan Ryan:

First	Last	Total 1-4
Nolan	Ryan	51.5
Tom	Seaver	46.1
Greg	Maddux	45.3
Jim	Palmer	45.2
Bob	Gibson	44.0
Sandy	Koufax	40.5
Roger	Clemens	38.7
Don	Sutton	37.9
Gaylord	Perry	36.3
Steve	Carlton	36.2

Our leaders' list is now a Hall of Famers' competition. The pretenders have gone home. Dick Stigman somehow managed to win only 3 of 21 games, given four runs to work with:

First	Last	Games	Team W	Team L	Gain	Won	Lost
Dick	Stigman	21	3	18	-8.1	3	6
Brett	Tomko	36	11	25	-8.0	8	17
Woodie	Fryman	41	14	27	-7.6	10	12

While Jeff Suppan Sandwiches has moved to the bottom of the summary competition:

First	Last	Total 1-4
Jeff	Suppan	-14.5
Livan	Hernandez	-14.0
Jeff	Weaver	-14.0

Suppan was 4-35 with one run—average performance—but was 6-31 with two runs (-3 games), 14-33 with three runs (-4), and 25-36 with four runs (-7), quietly drifting to the very back of the list. Working with five runs, Tom Seaver returns to the top:

First	Last	Games	Team W	Team L	Gain	Won	Lost
Tom	Seaver	78	62	16	12.0	51	7
Don	Drysdale	56	47	9	11.1	37	3
Whitey	Ford	39	36	3	11.0	27	2
Randy	Johnson	75	58	17	9.9	45	9
Warren	Spahn	44	38	6	9.8	30	3
Sandy	Koufax	38	34	4	9.6	22	1
Don	Sutton	77	59	18	9.6	48	9
Bert	Blyleven	90	67	23	9.3	52	13
Phil	Niekro	84	63	21	9.1	49	8
Tom	Glavine	81	61	20	9.1	49	12

And this puts Seaver back in the driver's seat in the overall competition:

First	Last	Total 1-5
Tom	Seaver	58.1
Nolan	Ryan	56.5
Jim	Palmer	53.3
Greg	Maddux	53.0
Sandy	Koufax	50.1
Don	Sutton	47.5
Roger	Clemens	46.7
Bob	Gibson	45.7
Whitey	Ford	45.2
Steve	Carlton	44.8

Mark Clark, Aaron Cook and Brian Anderson managed to lose consistently with five runs of support:

First	Last	Games	Team W	Team L	Gain	Won	Lost
Mark	Clark	29	10	19	-8.6	8	12
Aaron	Cook	24	8	16	-7.4	7	6
Brian	Anderson	30	12	18	-7.2	8	9

Which puts Anderson in last place overall:

First	Last	Total 1-5
Brian	Anderson	-20.2
Jason	Johnson	-18.7
Steve	Trachsel	-17.8

You will notice, however, that some of the totals are getting smaller. At two, three and four runs, the leading pitchers were 20 games better than average. At five runs, this number dropped to 12, and at six runs, it will drop to single digits:

First	Last	Games	Team W	Team L	Gain	Won	Lost
Roger	Clemens	70	59	11	8.1	43	0
Jim	Bunning	51	45	6	7.9	35	3
Steve	Carlton	65	55	10	7.7	43	4
Mike	Mussina	59	50	9	7.1	40	3
Whitey	Ford	44	39	5	7.0	31	0
Jim	Palmer	47	41	6	6.8	29	2
Bob	Gibson	39	35	4	6.6	31	3
Jack	Morris	52	44	8	6.2	39	2
Ferguson	Jenkins	41	36	5	6.2	27	4
Rudy	May	30	28	2	6.2	15	0

Clemens had 70 games with six runs, still a very large number, but the "advantage/disadvantage" numbers are shrinking rapidly because the overall winning percentage is approaching 1.000. Clemens was 43-0 when the team scored six runs, but then, the overall winning percentage for starting pitchers working with six runs was .815. Starting pitchers don't lose a lot of games when the team scores six. Although Mark Davis' teams lost a lot:

First	Last	Games	Team W	Team L	Gain	Won	Lost
Mark	Davis	13	3	10	-6.5	2	0
Joe	Kennedy	17	6	11	-6.4	4	4
Terry	Mulholland	36	20	16	-6.2	15	6

Mark Davis was 5-17 as a starting pitcher in 1984, and there are ten losses here that didn't go to him as a starter. But he moved to the bullpen and won a Cy Young Award as a reliever. With time running out, Tom Seaver solidifies his hold on the top spot:

First	Last	Total 1-6
Tom	Seaver	63.9
Jim	Palmer	60.2
Nolan	Ryan	58.9
Greg	Maddux	58.0
Roger	Clemens	54.8
Sandy	Koufax	53.8
Don	Sutton	53.5
Steve	Carlton	52.5
Bob	Gibson	52.3
Whitey	Ford	52.2

While Jason Johnson has taken over the bottom:

First	Last	Total 1-6
Jason	Johnson	-24.2
Brian	Anderson	-19.2
Joe	Kennedy	-18.8

Working with seven runs, the number one pitcher was Jim Kaat, whose teams were 44-2 at that level:

First	Last	Games	Team W	Team L	Gain	Won	Lost
Jim	Kaat	46	44	2	7.1	24	2
Randy	Johnson	43	40	3	5.5	31	1
Greg	Maddux	43	40	3	5.5	35	1
Mike	Cuellar	31	30	1	5.1	23	0
Ken	Hill	30	29	1	4.9	22	0
Don	Sutton	59	52	7	4.7	38	4
Bert	Blyleven	43	39	4	4.5	30	1
Tommy	John	49	43	5	4.5	28	0
Tom	Seaver	53	47	6	4.5	41	0
Charlie	Hough	37	34	3	4.3	28	1

Ken Hill? And look; Mike Cuellar is back. The bigger tranches are more reliable, but the smaller ones are more fun. Seaver, showing up on the leader's list once again, pulls five games ahead in the overall competition:

First	Last	Total 1-7
Tom	Seaver	68.4
Greg	Maddux	63.5
Jim	Palmer	63.1
Nolan	Ryan	59.4
Don	Sutton	58.1
Whitey	Ford	56.0
Roger	Clemens	55.2
Sandy	Koufax	52.9
Bob	Gibson	52.7
Steve	Carlton	52.5

On the other end, Steve Trachsel's teams lost 15 times when they scored 7 runs in a game:

First	Last	Games	Team W	Team L	Gain	Won	Lost
Steve	Trachsel	34	19	15	-8.3	15	4
Sidney	Ponson	32	20	12	-5.7	13	9
Jaime	Navarro	24	15	9	-4.3	11	4

Which puts Trachsel—and Sir Sidney—into the competition for the position as furthest below average:

First	Last	Total 1-7
Jason	Johnson	-23.8
Steve	Trachsel	-23.4
Sidney	Ponson	-23.4

OK, one more precinct to look at. These were the leading pitchers when the team scored 8 runs, or more than 8:

First	Last	Games	Team W	Team L	Gain	Won	Lost
Ferguson	Jenkins	92	91	1	7.6	74	0
Jamie	Moyer	125	120	5	6.6	92	0
Luis	Tiant	82	81	1	6.6	59	0
Bob	Gibson	63	62	0	5.8	51	0
Andy	Pettitte	94	91	3	5.8	79	1
Pedro	Martinez	71	70	1	5.6	57	0
Jimmy	Key	68	67	1	5.3	61	1
Curt	Schilling	76	74	2	5.1	61	0
Randy	Johnson	108	103	5	5.1	88	2
Jim	Palmer	86	83	3	5.0	68	1

While Pedro Astacio's teams lost 13 times with 8 runs or more. And there's Jason Johnson again:

First	Last	Games	Team W	Team L	Gain	Won	Lost
Pedro	Astacio	67	54	13	-6.8	42	7
Darren	Oliver	60	49	11	-5.4	34	4
Steve	Avery	50	40	10	-5.3	23	5
Kevin	Tapani	72	60	12	-5.3	47	4
Jason	Johnson	40	31	9	-5.3	25	4

Which makes Johnson the lowest-ranking pitcher of the last sixty years, by this method:

First	Last	Total 1-8
Jason	Johnson	-29.1
Steve	Trachsel	-23.0
Sidney	Ponson	-21.4

Johnson, with a career record of 56-100, was 22 full games (44 half-games) under .500. This method even somewhat understates how much damage he was really doing. Tom Seaver heads up the Hall of Famers:

First	Last	Total 1-8
Tom	Seaver	70.3
Jim	Palmer	68.1
Greg	Maddux	67.1
Nolan	Ryan	64.0
Whitey	Ford	60.1
Bob	Gibson	58.4
Don	Sutton	58.2
Roger	Clemens	57.6
Steve	Carlton	55.2
Sandy	Koufax	51.3

Seaver was 311-205 in his career, or 53 games over .500 (106 half-games). This method puts him at +70.

This method, the method that I have been using over the last few pages, incorporates and is thus vulnerable to park and era illusions. Tom Seaver looks a little bit better than he probably should because he pitched in a pitcher's park in an era when ERAs were relatively low. Clemens probably doesn't look quite as good as he was, because he pitched in a high-run era.

Our first method, however, is not necessarily vulnerable to those problems. In our other method, we are figuring the "effective runs allowed rate" for pitchers by looking at their ability to win with one run, two runs, three runs, etc. Of course, if a pitcher pitches in a hitter's park and in a hitter's era, his effective runs allowed rate will be different than if he had pitched in Dodger Stadium in 1965.

But in the comparison of John Burkett and Mike Morgan, for example, these issues are almost entirely irrelevant. Burkett and Morgan allowed essentially the same number of runs per nine innings. We then compare them on their ability to win with 1 run, 2 runs, 3 runs, etc. Let us suppose that one of these pitchers pitched for much better teams, got much better offensive support, and pitched in a much better pitcher's park. So what? It's not (really) relevant (it's marginally relevant for some minor issues). If pitcher A and pitcher B both allow 4.50 runs per game and are both working with 3 runs in a game, they should have the same ability to win, regardless of the park or the era in which they allowed these 4.50 runs and were supported by these 3 runs.

VII. Returning to Effective Runs Allowed

We are dealing here with the issue of whether some pitchers may have an ability to pitch especially well when they have an opportunity to win the game. We were working before with John Burkett, Mike Morgan and Whitey Ford, and let's throw Jim Clancy and Tom Seaver into the mix as well—Seaver, for obvious reasons, and Clancy, because he is the third man in the Burkett/Morgan comparison:

Pitcher	Innings	W	L	W pct	ERA	Total Runs Per 9 Innings
John Burkett	2648.1	166	136	.550	4.31	4.67
Jim Clancy	2517.1	140	167	.456	4.23	4.66
Mike Morgan	2772.1	141	186	.431	4.23	4.65

Working with one run of offensive support, Burkett's teams were 3-30, Clancy's were 3-37, Morgan's were 3-39, Ford's were 10-28, and Seaver's were 12-56:

First	Last	Games	Won	Lost	Effective Runs Allowed Rate	Effective Runs Allowed Rate
Whitey	Ford	39	10	28	64	1.67
Tom	Seaver	68	12	56	147	2.16
John	Burkett	33	3	30	104	3.16
Jim	Clancy	40	3	37	140	3.51
Mike	Morgan	42	3	39	151	3.61

Except that that's not *exactly* the method that I used in some cases. That's exactly the method I used for Clancy, Seaver and Morgan above, but not for Ford and Burkett.

We get into problems with small groups of data. Suppose that a pitcher went 0-12 when working with one run, or 0-1, or 0-39. What is his runs allowed rate? By the method above, you can't get an answer. You wind up searching for the square root of infinity, and, of course, only the Dalai Lama and Al Gore know what that is.

To prevent this from happening, I added "placekeeping data" to all groups of games involving less than 40 decisions. At one run, since the winning percentage of teams with one run was .101, I added one (placekeeping) win and nine losses—treating John Burkett as if he was 4-39, rather than 3-30, and Whitey Ford as if he was 11-37, rather than 10-28. These additions change the chart above to the following:

First	Last	Won	Lost	Effective Runs Allowed Rate	Effective Runs Allowed Rate
Whitey	Ford	10	28	70	1.83
Tom	Seaver	12	56	147	2.16
John	Burkett	3	30	103	3.12
Jim	Clancy	3	37	140	3.51
Mike	Morgan	3	39	151	3.61

I added these "placekeeping numbers" at all levels, to all pitchers who had less than 40 decisions at the level, always adding one "placekeeping win", but varying the number of losses as follows:

	Team Winning Percentage	Wins/Losses Added
1 Run	.101	1 and 9
2 Runs	.247	1 and 3
3 Runs	.389	1 and 1.6
4 Runs	.528	1 and .9
5 Runs	.641	1 and .56
6 Runs	.727	1 and .375
7 Run	.802	1 and .25
8 Runs or More	.907	1 and .1

These are the values for the five pitchers at the levels 2 runs and 3 runs:

First	Last	Won	Lost	TWO RUNS	
				Effective Runs Allowed Rate	Effective Runs Allowed Rate
Tom	Seaver	43	48	192	2.11
Whitey	Ford	19	22	88	2.15
John	Burkett	15	46	214	3.50
Jim	Clancy	8	36	187	4.24
Mike	Morgan	9	56	324	4.99

First	Last	Won	Lost	THREE RUNS	
				Effective Runs Allowed Rate	Effective Runs Allowed Rate
Whitey	Ford	45	30	184	2.45
Tom	Seaver	57	56	336	2.97
Jim	Clancy	29	40	243	3.52
Mike	Morgan	27	39	238	3.61
John	Burkett	24	37	227	3.72

Whitey Ford is doing really well here. Some people tend to think of Whitey Ford as a pitcher who won a lot of games because the Bronx Bombers scored seven runs a game for him. As the charts above show, this is anything but true. Ford won a lot of games 2-1, 3-1 and 3-2. This chart summarizes the three charts above:

First	Last	Won	Lost	TOTAL, ONE TO THREE RUNS	
				Effective Runs Allowed Rate	Effective Runs Allowed Rate
Whitey	Ford	74	80	342	2.22
Tom	Seaver	112	160	675	2.48
John	Burkett	42	113	544	3.51
Jim	Clancy	40	113	570	3.73
Mike	Morgan	39	134	714	4.13

In the other method, Seaver was number one because I was measuring the total distance away from an average pitcher, which gave Seaver an advantage over Ford because he had pitched 75 to 80% more games within our data. But on a per-game basis, Ford is more than holding his own. (The "Effective Runs Allowed" above are not actually integers, and may not add up exactly as you might expect for that reason.)

At the four-run level Seaver bests Ford and the three musketeers go Burkett-Morgan-Clancy, but the cumulative order stays the same:

First	Last	TOTALS AT FOUR RUNS				TOTAL, ONE TO FOUR RUNS			
		Won	Lost	Effective Runs Allowed	ERAR	Won	Lost	Effective Runs Allowed	ERAR
Whitey	Ford	35	25	203	3.38	109	105	544	2.54
Tom	Seaver	49	30	247	3.13	161	190	922	2.63
John	Burkett	25	25	200	4.00	67	138	744	3.63
Jim	Clancy	20	25	201	4.47	60	138	772	3.90
Mike	Morgan	24	25	200	4.08	63	159	914	4.12

Ford was the only one of these pitchers—and one of few pitchers in the study—who was able to deliver a winning record for his team in games with four runs or less. At the five-run level, Whitey Ford's teams were a fairly astonishing 36-3. Everybody was able to win over half the time with five runs, but Morgan's teams were only 29-23:

First	Last	TOTALS AT FIVE RUNS				TOTAL, ONE TO FIVE RUNS			
		Won	Lost	Effective Runs Allowed	ERAR	Won	Lost	Effective Runs Allowed	ERAR
Whitey	Ford	36	3	60	1.55	145	108	605	2.39
Tom	Seaver	62	16	198	2.54	223	206	1121	2.61
John	Burkett	28	14	148	3.54	95	152	892	3.61
Jim	Clancy	30	19	195	3.97	90	157	966	3.91
Mike	Morgan	29	23	232	4.45	92	182	1145	4.18

I mentioned earlier that Burkett was 18-4 when working with six runs, whereas Morgan was 16-4, which I represented as an advantage for Burkett. But actually, when we look at the team record, rather than the individual pitcher's won-lost record, Morgan beats Burkett at six runs. And Whitey Ford once again beats everybody:

		TOTALS AT SIX RUNS				TOTAL, ONE TO SIX RUNS			
First	Last	Won	Lost	Effective Runs Allowed	ERAR	Won	Lost	Effective Runs Allowed	ERAR
Whitey	Ford	39	5	95	2.15	184	113	699	2.36
Tom	Seaver	40	7	118	2.51	263	213	1239	2.60
John	Burkett	27	12	156	3.99	122	164	1048	3.66
Jim	Clancy	32	10	141	3.35	122	167	1107	3.83
Mike	Morgan	25	7	102	3.20	117	189	1248	4.08

At the seven-run level Jim Clancy's teams were 20-2, which is even better than Seaver's teams. But Ford's Yankees went 27-2:

		TOTALS AT SEVEN RUNS				TOTAL, ONE TO SEVEN RUNS			
First	Last	Won	Lost	Effective Runs Allowed	ERAR	Won	Lost	Effective Runs Allowed	ERAR
Whitey	Ford	27	2	58	1.98	211	115	757	2.32
Tom	Seaver	47	6	133	2.50	310	219	1371	2.59
John	Burkett	25	9	142	4.18	147	173	1190	3.72
Jim	Clancy	20	2	50	2.29	142	169	1157	3.72
Mike	Morgan	16	6	93	4.24	133	195	1341	4.09

We come, finally, to our last category, which is "eight runs or more". There's not much point in tracking it beyond eight runs because the winning percentages are getting so close to 1.000, but there is a difference between the "eight-run" category and the others, which is that up to now we have known *exactly* how many runs the team was working with on offense. We will assume that the offense, in those games in which it scores eight runs or more, averages nine runs.

Jim Clancy with eight runs or more was 40-1:

		TOTALS AT EIGHT RUNS				TOTAL, ONE OR MORE RUNS			
First	Last	Won	Lost	Effective Runs Allowed	ERAR	Won	Lost	Effective Runs Allowed	ERAR
Whitey	Ford	73	3	139	1.82	284	118	896	2.23
Tom	Seaver	59	4	148	2.34	369	223	1519	2.57
John	Burkett	77	6	209	2.51	224	179	1398	3.47
Jim	Clancy	40	1	58	1.42	182	170	1216	3.45
Mike	Morgan	48	7	189	3.44	181	202	1530	3.99

OK, I've got some housekeeping details to take care of here, but first let me say: I think that we have effectively demonstrated at this point—unless I am missing something—that Mike Morgan was not as effective a pitcher, in terms of delivering a *win*, as were Clancy and Burkett. In terms of ERA and runs allowed per nine innings, he was just the same. In terms of his effectiveness at delivering a win, given a certain number of runs to work with, he was *not* the same. We have done that, and we have created a framework for measuring the difference—measuring the costs to Mike Morgan's teams of his failure to respond to the situations. We'll pick up on those things in a moment.

The two housekeeping issues that we need to deal with are

1) What do we do with shutouts, and
2) Why are the "Effective Runs Allowed Rates" so low?

To this point we have not dealt with games in which the pitcher's team was shut out, because, if your team doesn't score any runs, it doesn't make any difference how well you pitch, you can't win. What can we do about these games?

There seem to be four options, which are:

1) To assume that every pitcher had the same level of effectiveness in these games—let's say 4.50 runs per game or something like that,
2) To assume that every pitcher had the same level of effectiveness in these games that he had overall,
3) To ignore them entirely, and
4) To ignore them entirely, except that we display them as losses.

I think the best option is (4)—to ignore them entirely, except that we display them as losses in the totals, so that we are displaying accurate totals of wins and losses for the starter's games.

The other question is, why are the Effective Runs Allowed Rates so low? Mike Morgan, after all, allowed 4.65 runs per nine innings in real life. We are saying here

1) That he was ineffective at pitching well when he had a chance to win, and yet
2) His "effective" runs allowed rate was 3.99.

What up with that?

Everybody is low. The reason for this is that the distribution curve of runs scored in a game (or runs allowed in a game) is asymmetrical. If teams average 4.00 runs in a game, they will never score less than zero, but they will sometimes score more than eight. That means that there have been more games with *less* than four than games with more than four, in order to re-balance the system at four.

The Pythagorean formula assumes that, when a team *averages* four runs a game, this is an average. In our study it is not an average; it is a constant. The "four" runs average for the four-run group is 4, 4, 4, 4, 4. But there will be more "opposing" games under 4.00 than over four, which means that there will be more wins than losses. If you take two teams which both average four runs a game head to head, but one team always scores exactly four but the other scores a varied number averaging four, the team that always scores four will win over half the time. The same is true at every level of offense, including one run. If a team always scored one run in every game and allowed an average of one run per game but in a varied pattern, they would win more than half their games.

This skews our calculations toward a lower-than-real-life effective runs allowed rate, and we'll need to adjust for that. It's actually kind of interesting how it happens. Remember this chart, which I presented earlier:

	Team Winning Percentage
0 Runs	.000
1 Run	.101
2 Runs	.247
3 Runs	.389
4 Runs	.528
5 Runs	.641
6 Runs	.727
7 Run	.802
8 Runs or More	.907

Based on that chart, we can figure what the "effective runs allowed rate" being calculated at each level of offensive effectiveness is:

	Team Winning Percentage	Effective Runs Allowed Rate
0 Runs	.000	
1 Run	.101	2.98
2 Runs	.247	3.49
3 Runs	.389	3.76
4 Runs	.528	3.78
5 Runs	.641	3.74
6 Runs	.727	3.68
7 Run	.802	3.48
8 Runs or More	.907	2.88

Again, when teams score 8 runs or more, we assume that they have scored an average of nine.

Anyway, the average runs allowed rate in this study was about 3.50 runs per game, whereas it should have been about 4.40. It's 21.4% low. We can correct for this, then, by multiplying the Effective Runs Allowed Rates calculated before by 14, and dividing by 11.

OK, picking up the "summary" chart before, but incorporating those two changes, this would be the data for the five gentlemen that we have been following here:

		FINAL DATA			
First	Last	Games	Team Wins	Team Losses	Effective Runs Allowed Rate
Whitey	Ford	423	284	139	2.84
Tom	Seaver	647	369	278	3.27
Jim	Clancy	380	182	198	4.40
John	Burkett	423	224	199	4.42
Mike	Morgan	411	181	230	5.08

NOTES:

1) Tom Seaver's Effective Runs Allowed Rate here is actually *higher* than his real-life runs allowed rate (3.15 runs per nine innings). Seaver ranked first in our earlier competition because Seaver pitched more games with a low ERA than any other modern-era pitcher—thus, he is going to do very well in any kind of a runs-allowed rate competition among modern pitchers.

2) Whitey Ford's Effective Runs Allowed Rate is the lowest of any pitcher in our study with a reasonable number of starts. Ford is number one on the list; Bryan Rekar is number 663.

3) Jim Clancy surged at the last minute in our data, pushing ahead of John Burkett. People assume that Mike Morgan pitched for terrible teams, although he actually didn't, on balance. Jim Clancy pitched for worse teams than Morgan did, but Clancy had a better won-lost record. If Clancy had matched the won-lost percentage of his team in every season, his career record would have been 154-161 (.489).

I'm not entirely happy with Clancy's evaluation. Clancy's teams went 40-1 when they scored eight runs or more, which creates a very low Effective Runs Allowed Rate for him in those games, but if his team's had gone, say, 38-3, then we would have a very different calculation for him in those games, driving his overall final figure up by 15 points to 4.55. The system allows a disproportionate impact of a very few games in that case, which it should not do; I should have devised some way to prevent that from happening. Charts sometimes act irrationally near their boundaries; you probably all know this.

VIII. Final Thoughts

In saying that Mike Morgan, for example, did not pitch well when he had chances to win ball games, in saying that, for example, Whitey Ford and Bob Gibson did, I am not offering a moral judgment. I have not established, and I am not saying, that these performance deviations are beyond what could have occurred by chance.

But I am saying that these performance anomalies are "real" in this sense: that wins and losses resulted from them, and that therefore we can and should appropriately consider this in evaluating these players.

Mike Morgan, I think, is shown as being 36 runs below average as a pitcher for his career. The real number, I would argue, is closer to minus 150. Morgan allowed 4.65 runs per nine innings—but he won ballgames with the consistency of a pitcher allowing 5.08 runs. That's a difference, over the course of his career, of 132 runs.

It is a truism among the gray that when we were young we knew everything. It is more true than normal in my case, because when I was young I actually DID know more about analyzing baseball statistics than anybody else did, except maybe Pete Palmer and Dick Cramer. Now, young analysts shoot by me so fast I don't even have time to genuflect.

That's fine; I enjoy trying to keep up. The thrust of modern baseball research is toward small-unit accomplishments (strikeouts, walks, home runs) and away from aggregates like wins, losses and ERA. That's fine, too; 35 years ago I was pushing to pay less attention to real-life data composites, and more to details. We may perhaps occasionally have overshot the mark.

RickieWikiLeaks

by Bill James

———·—

Whenever they say "WikiLeaks,"
I always think of Rickie Weeks;
You may call it treason,
But I call it a double play.

"Late" Careers

by Bill James

Spinning off the signing of Jayson Werth to a huge contract by the Nationals, there has been a thread in the "Hey, Bill" section of Bill James Online about players who had very "late" careers… players who were late getting a shot, but had good careers anyway. Here is a chronological chart of players who had (or are having) late careers, defined as "two-thirds of their career games played or more after the age of 30."

The categories of this chart are:

- Year—the year in which the player was 30 years old
- Years played in the majors by the age of 30
- Games played by the age of 30
- Career Home Runs by the age of 30
- Career RBI by the age of 30
- Career Batting Average by the age of 30
- Years played in the majors after the age of 30
- Games played in the majors after the age of 30
- Career Home Runs after the age of 30
- Career RBI after the age of 30
- Career Batting Average after the age of 30
- Percentage of career games that are after the age-30 season (Late Pct)

First	Last	YEAR	Years	G	HR	RBI	Avg	Years	G	HR	RBI	Avg	Late Pct
Deacon	White	1878	3	186	3	138	.348	12	1113	15	618	.295	86%
Jim	O'Rourke	1881	6	441	10	216	.315	13	1333	41	794	.308	75%
Cap	Anson	1882	7	488	5	404	.353	15	1788	92	1475	.322	79%
Dave	Foutz	1887	4	302	7	0	.296	9	833	24	548	.270	73%
Chief	Zimmer	1891	7	418	6	169	.235	12	862	20	451	.285	67%
Bones	Ely	1893	5	205	0	27	.240	9	1136	24	559	.261	85%
Frank	Bowerman	1899	5	226	4	108	.273	10	819	9	284	.243	78%
Jack	McCarthy	1899	4	364	7	188	.292	8	727	0	286	.284	67%
Doc	Casey	1900	3	172	1	61	.263	7	942	8	293	.258	85%
Jimmy	Austin	1910	2	269	3	75	.224	16	1311	10	315	.251	83%
Cy	Williams	1918	7	633	40	249	.256	12	1369	211	756	.308	68%
Ken	Williams	1920	5	289	16	125	.285	9	1108	180	788	.328	79%
Sam	Rice	1920	6	518	7	240	.319	14	1886	27	838	.323	78%
George	Harper	1922	4	288	2	99	.282	7	785	89	429	.310	73%
Sparky	Adams	1925	4	372	7	113	.284	9	1052	2	281	.286	74%
Rip	Radcliff	1936	3	298	18	155	.308	7	783	24	377	.312	72%
George	McQuinn	1940	4	491	48	273	.299	8	1059	87	521	.264	68%
Walker	Cooper	1945	6	437	30	241	.298	12	1036	143	571	.279	70%
Hank	Majeski	1947	5	355	16	154	.262	8	714	41	347	.289	67%
Hank	Sauer	1947	3	47	7	29	.290	12	1352	281	847	.266	97%
Jackie	Robinson	1949	3	454	40	257	.312	7	928	97	477	.311	67%
Dave	Philley	1950	6	606	21	228	.270	12	1298	63	501	.270	68%
Minnie	Minoso	1953	4	453	39	242	.305	13	1382	147	781	.296	75%
Jim	Rivera	1953	2	306	18	126	.256	8	865	65	296	.257	74%
Dale	Long	1956	3	323	46	182	.271	7	690	86	285	.264	68%
Elston	Howard	1959	5	533	52	260	.279	9	1072	115	502	.272	67%
Ed	Charles	1963	2	305	32	153	.277	6	700	54	268	.257	70%
Davey	Lopes	1975	4	453	24	114	.266	12	1359	131	500	.262	75%
Tom	Paciorek	1977	8	447	15	105	.254	10	945	71	398	.292	68%

The rapid expansion in the above era (1961-1977) appears to have prevented deserving players from being locked in the minors. Resuming the chart:

First	Last	YEAR	Years	G	HR	RBI	Avg	Years	G	HR	RBI	Avg	Late Pct
Mike	Easler	1981	8	339	31	136	.302	6	812	87	386	.290	71%
Ernie	Whitt	1982	6	318	19	101	.240	9	1010	115	433	.251	76%
Jim	Eisenreich	1989	6	308	16	111	.268	9	1114	36	366	.297	78%
Otis	Nixon	1989	7	506	3	55	.222	10	1203	8	263	.280	70%
Edgar	Martinez	1993	7	563	49	217	.306	11	1492	260	1044	.314	73%
Jeff	Reboulet	1994	3	256	5	54	.242	9	762	15	148	.240	75%
Jeff	Conine	1996	6	604	81	372	.298	11	1420	133	699	.279	70%
Matt	Stairs	1998	6	401	64	226	.288	11	1360	195	655	.258	77%
Orlando	Palmeiro	1999	5	323	1	59	.279	8	883	11	167	.272	73%
Scott	Hatteberg	2000	6	360	31	134	.273	8	954	75	393	.273	73%
Craig	Counsell	2001	6	457	11	116	.269	9	1060	30	265	.253	70%
Raul	Ibanez	2002	7	472	51	215	.270	8	1201	181	755	.288	72%
Paul	Lo Duca	2002	5	350	40	174	.290	6	732	40	307	.284	68%
Melvin	Mora	2002	4	475	34	160	.249	8	1039	137	578	.289	69%
Casey	Blake	2004	6	353	47	162	.261	6	849	116	428	.265	71%

The ultimate "late" career is Hank Sauer. Luke Easter is not on the list because I required a 1000-game career. Easter played only 491 major league games.

STINK-O-METER

by Bill James

The 2010 Pittsburgh Pirates had their 18th consecutive losing season, which—or so I am told—is an all-time record for an American sports franchise. A Pittsburgh sportswriter e-mailed me, asking me how I would compare this record of failure and frustration to others.

Well, how would we?

There are, in baseball history, many claimants to exceptional misery. The Mets of the 1960s. The St. Louis Browns. The Cleveland Indians of the '60s, '70s and '80s. The Boston Braves and Philadelphia Phillies of the 1930s. The Brooklyn Dodgers of the 1920s, the Daffiness Boys. The Washington Senators; First in War, First in Peace, Last in the American League. The Cubbies.

Everybody would prefer to win, but if you can't win, you might as well claim to be the Biggest Loser, no? We have a morbid attraction to suffering with baseball teams: it's not real suffering. It's annoying; it's not really painful. We enjoy kvetching about it—not as much as we would enjoy winning, true, but much more than we would enjoy spending the same number of years on Devil's Island or trying to keep track of Lindsay Lohan. But how do we sort out these competing claims and decide who the Losing Leaders really are?

The Pirates have had 18 straight losing seasons, yes, and this is certainly one valid measure of a team's level of futility. It's not the only one. The Pirates have lost 100 games in that stretch only twice. The Royals had a winning season in 2003, but they have also lost 100 games four times in recent years, and have lost 97 games or more seven times since 1999. Who is to say which is worse?

Let's take it on.

I figured a "Loser Score" for each franchise after each season in this way. If a team has a losing season, their Loser Score is:

- Their Loser Score total from the previous year, plus
- The number of games that they were under .500, plus
- The number of consecutive losing seasons for the franchise.

The Pirates after the 2008 season were at 451. In 2009 they finished 62-99, 37 games under .500, so we add 37 points for that. This was their 17th consecutive losing season, so we add another 17 points for that. That makes 505. In 2010 they were 48 games under .500, and that was their 18th consecutive beat-down, so there's another 66 points, which makes 571. The Pirates currently have a Loser Score of 571.

If a team has a non-losing season (.500 or above), their Loser Score is:

- Their Loser Score total from the previous year, minus
- The number of games that they were above .500, if any, times
- .90 if it was the first in the series, .80 if it was the second, .70 if it was the third, etc.,
- Converted into the nearest integer,
- But not less than zero,
- And all teams winning the World Series have a score of zero.

The Detroit Tigers after the 2005 season had a Loser Score of 465—about where the Pirates were in 2008. The Tigers had a great season in 2006 (95-67), which reduced their score to 391 (465, minus 10%, minus 28 because they were 28 games over .500). They had another winning season in 2007 (88-74), which reduced their Loser Score to 299 (391, minus 20% because it was their second consecutive non-losing season, minus 14 because they were 14 games over .500).

They reversed that record in 2008 (74-88), which moved them back up to 314 (299, plus 14, plus one for it being the first losing season of the sequence.) But they got back on the good side of the ledger in 2009 (86-77), which reduced their score to 274 (314, minus 10%, minus 9.) They played .500 ball in 2010 (81-81), which reduced their score by 20%, since it was their second consecutive non-losing season; they're down to 219.

Most teams have *some* Loser Score after every season; about 70% do. All of the losing teams in a season have Loser Scores greater than zero, while about 40% of the non-losing teams do, as well, carrying forward the burdens of past seasons not yet expiated. If the

Tigers just have a losing season, a winning season, a losing season, a winning season, etc., their Loser Score will atrophy within a few years, as the declines will be larger than the increases. A Loser Score of 219 is still fairly high, and the team won't stay at that level if they have even intermittent success.

OK, let's go back to 1876 and trace the evolution of the Loser Leader Lists.

The Early Years

In the first years of baseball history the title of baseball's biggest losers passed quickly from franchise to franchise, and, as these numbers weren't really based on much of anything, we'll pass over exactly who those were. The minimum Loser Score that is really significant is 100, and the first team to reach that level was the Philadelphia Phillies in 1884, after their second year in the National League. The Phillies finished 16-81 in 1883, which put them at 66, and then went 39-73 in 1884, which put them at 102. They had a higher score than the teams which had preceded them only because the schedule was growing longer.

In quick succession after that the Phillies were replaced by the Detroit Wolverines, the Baltimore Orioles, the Indianapolis Hoosiers, the Washington Statesmen and the Cleveland Spiders. All of this happened by 1892, and the highest score posted by 1892 was just 187.

The Colonels

Baseball's first true down-and-out, perennial doormat was the Louisville Colonels of the National League. The Colonels went 27-111 in 1889 and then, as most of the best players in the league left to start the Player's League, won the same league in 1890, going 87-43. That was a one-off, however, and the Colonels resumed their losing ways in 1891, finishing 30 games under .500 in 1891, 27 games in 1892, and 25 games in 1893.

That was sufficient to put them atop the loser's list by 1893, but with a Loser Score of just 157. Then they started to lose in earnest, going 35-94 in 1894, 35-95 in 1895, and 38-93 in 1896. By 1896 their Loser Score was up to 346, easily the highest in baseball history up to that time—and they were not finished. They finished 52-79 in 1897, 70-81 in 1898, and 75-77 in 1899.

By 1899, with a Loser Score of 410, the National League decided to put them out of their misery. The National League had 12 teams in 1899, but several of them were not competitive teams. They were, in essence, "feeder" teams. The League decided it was better off without them.

The Cardinals

While the Colonels had been the biggest losers of the 1890s, there was a competition. Close at their heels were the Washington Senators and the St. Louis Cardinals. By 1899 these were the "Loser Score standings":

1899	Louisville	Colonels	NL	410
1899	Washington	Senators	NL	379
1899	St. Louis	Cardinals	NL	301
1899	Cleveland	Spiders	NL	115

The league eliminated the Colonels, the Senators and the Spiders, and this left the Cardinals as the game's Big Losers. (The "115" for the Spiders, by the way, was all based on the 1899 season. The Spiders, who came into the 1899 season with a string of seven consecutive winning seasons, finished 114 games under .500, putting their score at 115.)

The Cardinals claimed the title by disqualification, but they held it on merit. The Cardinals—who had gone 29-102 in 1897 and 39-111 in 1898—lost 94 games in 1903, 96 in 1905, 98 in 1907, 101 in 1907, 105 in 1908, 98 in 1909, 90 in 1910, 90 in 1912, 99 in 1913, and 93 in 1916. Through all of this period, they kept a vice grip on the Biggest Loser title, expanding their lead throughout.

The Cardinals didn't merely lose; they embarrassed themselves, and embarrassed the city. Owners fought and feuded in the newspapers with managers they had hired, and with the owners of other teams. Owners fired managers for inane and improbable reasons. They were a true Busch League operation.

The record score on the Stink-O-Meter had been 410, by the Colonels in 1899. The Cardinals broke that record in 1906, reached 500 in 1907, reached 600 in 1909, and reached a peak of 663 in 1913.

From 1915 on, the runners up for the title were the Cardinals' roommate, the Browns:

1915	St. Louis	Cardinals	NL	598
1915	St. Louis	Browns	AL	382
1915	Brooklyn	Dodgers	NL	352

1918	St. Louis	Cardinals	NL	586
1918	St. Louis	Browns	AL	389
1918	Brooklyn	Dodgers	NL	274

1916	St. Louis	Cardinals	NL	633
1916	St. Louis	Browns	AL	340
1916	Brooklyn	Dodgers	NL	248

1919	St. Louis	Cardinals	NL	617
1919	St. Louis	Browns	AL	397
1919	Philadelphia	A's	AL	297

1917	St. Louis	Cardinals	NL	558
1917	St. Louis	Browns	AL	381
1917	Brooklyn	Dodgers	NL	260

1920	St. Louis	Cardinals	NL	624
1920	St. Louis	Browns	AL	402
1920	Philadelphia	A's	AL	361

By 1921 the Cardinals had been the Biggest Losers in baseball for more than twenty years—a very, very, long time. After that, you know what happened to them. It was Branch Rickey who finally managed the Cardinals out of the wilderness. In the early 1920s Rickey moved from the manager's job into the front office, invented the modern farm system, and lifted the Cardinals from the bottom of the National League to the top. By 1925 the Cardinals had cut their Loser Score to 280—still a very significant number, but 40% of what it had once been. They won the World Series in 1926, Alexander staggering out of the bullpen to strike out Lazzeri, and this wiped out their Loser Score, putting them at zero.

From then until now, the Cardinals have never been big losers. From 1926 until now, the highest Loser Score the Cardinal franchise has ever had was 39, in 1980—and 39 is nothing. The Cardinals have been up; they've been down—but they've never *really* been down again.

The Philadelphia A's

The Philadelphia Athletics, a championship operation up until 1914, sold off their stars to keep them in the American League, and lost 109 games in 1915, 117 in 1916. They lost 100-plus in 1919, and moved onto the list of baseball's biggest losers. They lost 100+ again in 1920.

In 1921 the Cardinals won 87 games, the most they had won since 1889. They followed this up with 85 more wins in 1922, Branch Rickey still in the manager's seat. The St. Louis Browns, with George Sisler and the all-time outfield of Baby Doll Jacobson, Jack Tobin and Ken Williams, had also moved into contention; they went

81-73, and 93-61 in 1922. The Athletics lost 100+ games for the third straight year in 1921, and so it was the A's, not the Browns, who descended to the Biggest Loser title once the Cardinals finally vacated.

The A's, however, had a fairly brief and undistinguished run at the bottom. The A's moved into the loser title seat in 1922 with a total of 447. They upped that to 470 in 1923 and 490 in 1924, but Connie Mack was re-building. Adding Lefty Grove, Mickey Cochrane, Jimmie Foxx and other stars, Mack had the A's over .500 in 1925, and out of the hot seat in 1926.

The Phillies, Part II

Though never really a powerhouse, the Phillies—the Big Losers of 1884—had wiped clean their loser slate by 1888 and kept their count at zero most of the time from 1888 into the twentieth century. A series of three bad seasons after the start of the century drove their Loser Score up to 116, but the arrival of Pete Alexander had returned them to zero by 1915.

After the 1917 season the Phillies, in a deal that presaged the sale of Babe Ruth to the Yankees, sold Alex to the Cubs for $55,000 and three minor players. The Phillies began now a run of the ugliest seasons in modern baseball history: 47-90 in 1919, 62-91 in 1920, 51-103 in 1922, 57-96 in 1922, 50-104 in 1923, 55-96 in 1924, 58-93 in 1926, 51-103 in 1927, 43-109 in 1928, and 52-102 in 1930.

Meanwhile, the history of the Boston Red Sox in this era was running parallel. The sale of Babe Ruth by the Red Sox was, in reality, only one of a long, long series of sales of quality players to better teams by the Red Sox, the Phillies and some other teams. These teams, to be blunt, had quit on their fans. They had no intention of winning anything, and they now entered a period of failure so dark that they considered farts to be echo location. Sorry. By 1926 these were the Loser Leaders:

1926	Philadelphia	Phillies	NL	368
1926	Philadelphia	A's	AL	318
1926	Boston	Braves	NL	264
1926	St. Louis	Browns	AL	256
1926	Boston	Red Sox	AL	255

The Red Sox lost 103 games in 1927; the Braves lost 103 in 1928, and by 1928 these were the standings:

1928	Philadelphia	Phillies	NL	507
1928	Boston	Red Sox	AL	365
1928	Boston	Braves	NL	364
1928	St. Louis	Browns	AL	254
1928	Brooklyn	Dodgers	NL	169

That's the Daffiness Boys in Brooklyn, Wilbert Robinson's famed losers with Babe Herman, Rube Bressler, and the ancient Max Carey. They were never really big losers; they were sort of Also-Ran Losers whose failings were exaggerated by the Damon Runyan press corps because New Yorkers always have to believe they have the best of everything, even Losers. In 1930 the Phillies and Red Sox lost 102 games apiece, and by 1931 the standings were:

1931	Philadelphia	Phillies	NL	629
1931	Boston	Red Sox	AL	517
1931	Boston	Braves	NL	473
1931	St. Louis	Browns	AL	254
1931	Chicago	White Sox	AL	180

The Phillies were now closing in on the historic levels of ineptitude mapped out by the Cardinals twenty years earlier. The Cardinals had peaked at 663 in 1913.

In 1932 the Phillies had a "good" year, a "winning" season. With Chuck Klein winning the National League Triple Crown, the Phillies won 78 games, and lost only 76. The Red Sox, meanwhile, went 43-111, and moved to the top of the list:

1932	Boston	Red Sox	AL	599
1932	Philadelphia	Phillies	NL	564
1932	Boston	Braves	NL	426
1932	St. Louis	Browns	AL	285
1932	Chicago	White Sox	AL	239

The Red Sox

In February, 1933, however, Tom Yawkey bought the Red Sox. Yawkey immediately began spending money to bring players to the Red Sox, rather than selling them off as had been the practice of Red Sox owners since 1918. The Red Sox spent only one more year at the head of the list (1933), and then began to make progress on paying off their Loser Debt. Their Loser Score was under 300 by 1938, under 100 by 1940, and was off the books by 1942.

The Red Sox didn't become significant losers again until the post-Ted Williams years in the early 1960s, when their Loser Score reached as high as 165 in 1966. They had cleaned that off again by 1972, and the Red Sox Loser Score has not been higher than 31 since 1972.

The Phillies, Part III

After the one winning season in 1932, however, the Phillies resumed their pagan ways. They lost 92 games in 1933, 93 games in 1934. In 1936 they were 54-100.

The Phillies were still back there, where the Red Sox had been in the 1920s, selling off their best players. Dolph Camilli hit .339 for them in 1937, had an OPS over 1.000 in '36 and '37. They sold him to the Dodgers for $45,000, and he won an MVP Award for the Dodgers. They picked up Bucky Walters, a failed infielder, as a pitcher. He turned out to be a pretty fair pitcher, so they sold him to Cincinnati for $50,000, and he won an MVP Award for the Reds. The Phillies went 45-105 in 1938, 45-106 in 1939, 50-103 in 1940, 43-111 in 1941, and 42-109 in 1942.

One of the central questions of this article is, "Which team really was the Biggest Loser in baseball history?" Well, the Phillies of 1918-1948 were the Biggest Losers in baseball history—by far. Nobody else is in the game with them. The Pirates may have had 18 straight losing seasons, but the Phillies lost 14 straight, had one "winning" season (78-76) and then had 16 straight losing seasons after that—30 losing seasons in 31 years, many of them absolutely awful. They had five straight seasons (1938-1942) far worse than anything the Pirates had suffered until 2010—those five, and many others. They lost 108 games again in 1945. This chart tracks the Phillies' Loser Score from 1917 to 1948:

Year	Team	W	L	Pct	Loser Score	Year	Team	W	L	Pct	Loser Score
1917	Phillies	87	65	.572	0	1933	Phillies	60	92	.395	597
1918	Phillies	55	68	.447	14	1934	Phillies	56	93	.376	636
1919	Phillies	47	90	.343	59	1935	Phillies	64	89	.418	664
1920	Phillies	62	91	.405	91	1936	Phillies	54	100	.351	714
1921	Phillies	51	103	.331	147	1937	Phillies	61	91	.401	749
1922	Phillies	57	96	.373	191	1938	Phillies	45	105	.300	815
1923	Phillies	50	104	.325	251	1939	Phillies	45	106	.298	883
1924	Phillies	55	96	.364	299	1940	Phillies	50	103	.327	944
1925	Phillies	68	85	.444	324	1941	Phillies	43	111	.279	1021
1926	Phillies	58	93	.384	368	1942	Phillies	42	109	.278	1098
1927	Phillies	51	103	.331	430	1943	Phillies	64	90	.416	1135
1928	Phillies	43	109	.283	507	1944	Phillies	61	92	.399	1178
1929	Phillies	71	82	.464	530	1945	Phillies	46	108	.299	1253
1930	Phillies	52	102	.338	593	1946	Phillies	69	85	.448	1283
1931	Phillies	66	88	.429	629	1947	Phillies	62	92	.403	1328
1932	Phillies	78	76	.506	564	1948	Phillies	66	88	.429	1366

The Phillies became the biggest losers in baseball history in 1935, when their Loser Score reached 664, breaking the record 663 set 22 years earlier by the Cardinals. The Phillies' score would grow to almost twice that number, 1366. No other team in baseball history has approached that standard. If the Pirates were to lose 100 games a year from now on, they wouldn't match the Phillies' misery until 2023.

It is just a theory, but it may be these years, in which not only were the Phillies awful but the Philadelphia A's often were matching them loss for loss…it may be this era that shaped the character of the Philadelphia sports fans, who later became famous for booing Santa Claus. The Philadelphia fans were notoriously negative, yes, but you might be, too, if you had to watch 51 losing teams in 31 years (30 by the Phillies, 21 by the Athletics), with almost half of those teams losing 100 games.

Bob Carpenter bought the Phillies in 1943, and, as Yawkey had done with the Red Sox ten years earlier, began to build them into a competitive franchise. It took several years. It was harder to get off the floor in 1943 than it had been in 1933, because baseball was better organized. By the 1940s teams had farm systems—the other teams did—and, as the Phillies were the last team to make a business out of selling their young players to their competitors, once they got out of the business, there was nobody left to buy from. They had to build. By 1946 the Phillies were getting better; in 1949 they actually had a winning record, and in 1950, of course, the Phillies won the National League pennant.

It would take a little longer for them to move out of the Big Loser chair. These were the standings in 1935, in 1940, in 1945, and 1948:

1935	Philadelphia	Phillies	NL	664
1935	Boston	Red Sox	AL	455
1935	St. Louis	Browns	AL	381
1935	Chicago	White Sox	AL	329
1935	Boston	Braves	NL	303

1940	Philadelphia	Phillies	NL	944
1940	St. Louis	Browns	AL	656
1940	Philadelphia	A's	AL	299
1940	Boston	Braves	NL	271
1940	Chicago	White Sox	AL	141

1945	Philadelphia	Phillies	NL	1253
1945	Philadelphia	A's	AL	531
1945	Boston	Braves	NL	416
1945	St. Louis	Browns	AL	409
1945	Chicago	White Sox	AL	116

1948	Philadelphia	Phillies	NL	1366
1948	St. Louis	Browns	AL	508
1948	Philadelphia	A's	AL	416
1948	Chicago	White Sox	AL	198
1948	Washington	Senators	AL	183

It's like being sprayed by a skunk. The Phillies had been sprayed by the Great Skunk in the Sky so thoroughly and for so long that it would take several years of bathing in tomato juice to get rid of it. But by 1952 these were the standings:

1952	Philadelphia	Phillies	NL	841
1952	St. Louis	Browns	AL	692
1952	Philadelphia	A's	AL	311
1952	Washington	Senators	AL	270
1952	Cincinnati	Reds	NL	206

The Phillies won 83 games in 1953 (83-71), and, by 1953, the St. Louis Browns' moment had finally arrived.

The Artists Once Known as the St. Louis Browns

The irony being, of course, that they were no longer the Browns. The Browns lost 100 games in 1953, which wasn't an unusual thing for them, but with the Phillies no longer reeking, the Browns were finally able to claim the title as baseball's Biggest Losers:

1953	St. Louis	Browns	AL	746
1953	Philadelphia	Phillies	NL	661
1953	Philadelphia	A's	AL	348
1953	Pittsburgh	Pirates	NL	259
1953	Cincinnati	Reds	NL	233

That winter the St. Louis Browns became the Baltimore Orioles. We are regarding this here as one franchise. We are carrying over the Loser Score of the St. Louis Browns to Baltimore, understanding of course that this is merely one option, and that it could have been done some other way.

The Orioles lost 100 games in 1954, but, under the leadership of Paul Richards, they also began to make some progress, losing 97 games in 1955 but only 85 in 1956. These were the Biggest Loser standings post-1956:

1956	Baltimore	Orioles	AL	878
1956	Philadelphia	Phillies	NL	613
1956	Kansas City	A's	AL	487
1956	Pittsburgh	Pirates	NL	384
1956	Washington	Senators	AL	328

The Phillies, playing about .500 ball, still carried some of the burdens of the dreadful era which had ended eight years earlier. The Orioles had a .500 season in 1957, but then lost again in 1958 and 1959, leaving:

1959	Baltimore	Orioles	AL	804
1959	Philadelphia	Phillies	NL	597
1959	Kansas City	A's	AL	570
1959	Washington	Senators	AL	447
1959	Chicago	Cubs	NL	297

The "878" score rung down by the Browns/Orioles was, at that time, the second-highest figure in baseball history. As was true for the Phillies, it would take a while to wash that away. In 1960 the Orioles, with an almost all-rookie lineup, won 89 games—but held on to the top spot:

1960	Baltimore	Orioles	AL	700
1960	Philadelphia	Phillies	NL	636
1960	Kansas City	A's	AL	616
1960	Washington	Senators	AL	462
1960	Chicago	Cubs	NL	339

In 1961, however, the Orioles won 95 games, and shed the label as baseball's Biggest Losers. A series of good seasons followed. Led by Brooks Robinson and Boog Powell, the Orioles by 1965 had cut their Loser Score to 219, escaping the list, and their 1966 World Series victory wiped out their debt, making the franchise Loser-Free, literally for the first time ever. The Browns had had a losing record in their first season, and until 1966 had never gotten all the way back to zero.

The Phillies, Part IV

The Phillies, meanwhile, had let their subscription to *Winners Monthly* expire, and had fallen back into their old ways. They lost 85 games in 1958 (69-85), 90 games in 1959, and 95 in 1960. There was a symmetry about it: one could see one hundred losses coming, but what came was much worse. The Phillies, now managed by Gene Mauch, were 30-64 on July 28, 1961, on target for 100+ losses, but then they lost 23 straight games, dropping to 30-87. They managed to win some games in August and September, but they still finished the 1961 season at 47-107. This put them back atop the Loser List:

1961	Philadelphia	Phillies	NL	700
1961	Kansas City	A's	AL	664
1961	Baltimore	Orioles	AL	532
1961	Minnesota	Twins	AL	490
1961	Chicago	Cubs	NL	374

But this time, the stay was mercifully brief. The Phillies won 82 games in 1962, while their old partners in grime, the Athletics, continued to lose. The Phillies under Gene Mauch, adding Dick Allen in 1964, began to win regularly, and by 1968 had reduced their Loser Score to a mere 3 points. One more 82-80 season, and they'd have been free and clear.

The Phillies's history has remained rocky. They have had more difficult periods. Their Loser Score has gone as high as 222 (2000). But they have also had periods of success, including obviously recently, and their slate is clean at this writing.

The Kansas City A's

The Kansas City A's, of course, were the team of my childhood. As the Damon Runyan crowd liked to squawk about the Dodgers, as the New York media of the 1960s liked to squeal about the Mets, I take a perverse pride in moaning about the Kansas City A's. I survived Charlie Finley. Do I get a T-Shirt or something?

As the Baltimore Orioles had begun life with the debts of their fathers, the St. Louis Browns, so too the Kansas City A's had been burdened with the sins of Connie Mack's dotage.

The Orioles, however, took on the challenge and made something of themselves. The A's in K.C. picked up the bells and greasepaint of their ancestors and became the laughingstock of baseball.

The A's moved to Kansas City in 1954 with a Loser Score of 402. In their thirteen years in Kansas City, they never came close to playing .500 baseball. This chart tracks the Trail of Tears between their departure from Philadelphia and their arrival in Oakland:

Year	Post	Team	League	Wins (if any)	Losses	Pct.	Loser Score
1955	Kansas City	A's	AL	63	91	.409	433
1956	Kansas City	A's	AL	52	102	.338	487
1957	Kansas City	A's	AL	59	94	.386	527
1958	Kansas City	A's	AL	73	81	.474	541
1959	Kansas City	A's	AL	66	88	.429	570
1960	Kansas City	A's	AL	58	96	.377	616
1961	Kansas City	A's	AL	61	100	.379	664
1962	Kansas City	A's	AL	72	90	.444	692
1963	Kansas City	A's	AL	73	89	.451	719
1964	Kansas City	A's	AL	57	105	.352	779
1965	Kansas City	A's	AL	59	103	.364	836
1966	Kansas City	A's	AL	74	86	.462	862
1967	Kansas City	A's	AL	62	99	.385	914

The 914 Loser Score compiled by the Kansas City A's (1955-1967) was then and remains now the second-highest such score to be found in baseball history.

There is, however, another way to look at the issue. Of the 914 points we have credited to the Kansas City A's, 512 were earned in Kansas City, but 402 were bequeathed to them by the sufferers of Philadelphia. When the Washington Senators moved to Minnesota in 1961, the American League announced that the franchise records would stay with the team in Washington, with a new Washington Senators franchise. Historians have largely ignored this edict, and with good reason. We don't work for those people. They get to decide what they get to decide. We do not and should not cede to them the decisions that are naturally ours.

It is as reasonable to regard the new Washington Senators as a continuation of the old as it is to do it the other way. The old Senators had a long losing tradition behind them, and the new Senators were pretty good Losers, themselves. If we regarded the new Senators as a continuation of the old, the A's would still outpoint them as the biggest losers of the era. However, if we regarded the Senators as a continuation and the A's as a new franchise beginning in 1955, then the Senators, not the A's, would be atop these three lists:

1962	Kansas City	A's	AL	692
1962	Philadelphia	Phillies	NL	629
1962	Baltimore	Orioles	AL	541
1962	Chicago	Cubs	NL	428
1962	Minnesota	Twins	AL	421

1965	Kansas City	A's	AL	836
1965	Chicago	Cubs	NL	414
1965	New York	Mets	NL	268
1965	Minnesota	Twins	AL	247
1965	Baltimore	Orioles	AL	219
1965	Washington	Senators	AL	205

1967	Kansas City	A's	AL	914
1967	Chicago	Cubs	NL	402
1967	New York	Mets	NL	348
1967	Washington	Senators	AL	244
1967	Houston	Astros	NL	187

The Athletics, of course, are the yo-yos of baseball history. Every twenty years or so, in Philadelphia and Oakland, the A's have put together an awesome team. Between these awesome moments, they generally couldn't beat David Spade's Celebrity All-Stars.

The Artists Once Known as the Washington Senators

The very moment that the A's left Kansas City they began to win again, which proves, I suppose, that it wasn't them, it was us. They had winning seasons in '68, '69 and '70, but they had been 512 points ahead (or is it behind?) in the Loser Race, and also, look at the list above. In second place were the Cubs, and in third place the Mets. Both teams got much better about the same time the A's did. As the A's tried to escape the Biggest Loser position, the two teams behind them melted away, unwilling to assume the crown. By 1970 the A's were nowhere near 912 points, but they were still in first place:

1970	Oakland	A's	AL	434
1970	Washington	Senators	AL	268
1970	Houston	Astros	NL	196
1970	Chicago	Cubs	NL	113
1970	Chicago	White Sox	AL	110

In 1971, however, the A's won 101 games, allowing the new Senators to slip into the first chair:

1971	Washington	Senators	AL	302
1971	Oakland	A's	AL	219
1971	Houston	Astros	NL	202
1971	San Diego	Padres	NL	139
1971	Philadelphia	Phillies	NL	129

The Senators, of course, are like the St. Louis Browns; as soon as they reached the top of the Loser List, they skipped town. From 1972 through 1976, the Texas Rangers ranked as the Biggest Losers in baseball:

1976	Texas	Rangers	AL	373
1976	San Diego	Padres	NL	326
1976	Milwaukee	Brewers	AL	230
1976	Montreal	Expos	NL	216
1976	California	Angels	AL	159

But you will note what has happened here. In 1962 the Twins ranked as the fifth-biggest losers in baseball, at 421 points (based largely on their accomplishments when disguised as the Washington Senators). By the 1970s the 400s had disappeared, and 160 points would put you on the leaders list. This was probably caused, in the main, by the Amateur Draft, which started in 1965. The June draft spread around the talent, a little, and allowed the worst teams to improve more rapidly, thus bringing about an era of comparatively good competitive balance. The Biggest Losers post-1965 did not approach the standards of those pre-1965.

The Padres

With better competitive balance the loser scores were lower, but the Padres still ruled the outhouse for seven years, 1977-1983.

1977	San Diego	Padres	NL	359
1977	Texas	Rangers	AL	310
1977	Milwaukee	Brewers	AL	267
1977	Montreal	Expos	NL	237
1977	California	Angels	AL	180

In 1977 three of the top four spots were occupied by teams from the 1969 expansion—the Expos, Padres and Brewers. By 1982 the teams from the 1977 expansion (Toronto and Seattle) were pushing toward the top:

1982	San Diego	Padres	NL	353
1982	Toronto	Blue Jays	AL	239
1982	Seattle	Mariners	AL	206
1982	New York	Mets	NL	206
1982	Texas	Rangers	AL	180
1982	Chicago	Cubs	NL	167

The Padres played .500 ball again in 1983, which did not cost them their spot on the list. But in 1984, of course, the Padres were in the World Series, which did:

1984	Seattle	Mariners	277
1984	Texas	Rangers	216
1984	Cleveland	Indians	203
1984	New York	Mets	197
1984	San Diego	Padres	175

The Mariners

OK, by 1984 the Mariners were the chiefs of Tribe Loser, but the score needed to keep them in that spot was now down to less than 300. But the Mariners had losing records for the next six seasons, which gave them a much more impressive total:

1990	Seattle	Mariners	AL	443
1990	Atlanta	Braves	NL	308
1990	Cleveland	Indians	AL	298
1990	Texas	Rangers	AL	177
1990	Chicago	Cubs	NL	162

With free agency, baseball was beginning—but just beginning—to re-segregate into winning and losing franchises. "Winning" seasons by the Mariners in 1991 and 1993 did not get them off the top of the list; they went just 83-79 in 1991, 82-80 in 1993, and lost almost a hundred in 1992. By 1996 the Mariners had been the Biggest Losers in baseball for 13 years, which actually is a very impressive accomplishment—one of the longest runs atop the Loser Board that any team has ever had. But the Mariners were not really BIG losers; they were just never quite good enough to stop their friends from flashing the Loser sign behind their backs:

1996	Seattle	Mariners	269
1996	Chicago	Cubs	163
1996	Detroit	Tigers	135
1996	Philadelphia	Phillies	122
1996	New York	Mets	119

The Mariners of 1996 were actually very much like the Tampa Bay Rays of today. Years of bottom-dwelling had given them years of high draft picks, which they had used to pile up a truly impressive list of players: Alex Rodriguez, Ken Griffey Jr., Edgar Martinez, Jay Buhner and Randy Johnson. By 1996 these players were coming together, and in 1997, the Mariners dropped out of the Skunk Chair:

1997	Chicago	Cubs	191
1997	Seattle	Mariners	170
1997	Philadelphia	Phillies	152
1997	Detroit	Tigers	143
1997	San Diego	Padres	116

The Cubs

In 1997 the Cubs were the Biggest Losers in baseball with a Loser Score of just 191—the lowest score for that title holder in more than 100 years. The amateur draft, up to that point, was still doing a very effective job of stirring the pot, keeping the same teams from settling on the bottom for long periods of time.

The Cubs are among baseball's most famous Losers. It is almost a word-association test; I say "Cubs", you say "Lovable Losers." And yet, up until 1997, the Cubs had never ranked at the top of our list—and even then it's with a piddly-ass score of 191. Should we be puzzled by this?

The Cubs up to 1945 were a strong franchise, with no losing tradition at all. From 1947 to 1962 they had fifteen losing seasons in sixteen years, building up a Loser Score of 428, which is very high although it was only the fourth-highest in baseball at that moment. It's higher than where the Kansas City Royals are today, and I will tell you this: that is not a fun territory.

By the late 1960s, however, the Durocher/Jenkins Cubs were

whittling away at this monument, and—like Gene Mauch's Phillies, but four years later—they would come very close to clearing the books. By 1972 they had reduced their Loser Score to 9 points. Since 1947, this is the Cubs' Loser Score in three-year increments:

Year	Loser Score
1947	17
1949	80
1952	130
1955	195
1958	284
1961	374
1964	394
1967	402
1970	113
1973	14
1976	77
1979	78
1982	167
1985	151
1988	197
1991	170
1994	171
1997	191
2000	218
2003	176
2006	162
2009	49
2010	62

The Cubs failures in the years 1947-1967, when those in my generation were gerbils, established the Cubbies as perpetual losers in our minds. The Cubs have never been at the top of the Lost Children List except one year, yes, and they have not equaled the Loss Logs of the Phillies or others, it is true.

But a Loser Score over 100 is a significant score. Usually twenty, twenty-five percent of the teams, at any moment, are over 100. The Cubs have been over 100 almost continuously since 1950. They've come close to squaring their accounts a couple of times, yes, but they haven't done it. They haven't won a World Series. Many teams have been able to clear their accounts without winning a World Series; the Cubs never have. There is very good reason to think of the Cubs the way we do.

The Tigers

The Detroit Tigers began play in 1901. In their first 50 years, and a little more, the Tigers had never had a Loser Score as high as 100. After some poor seasons in the early 1950s (1951-54) their score reached up to 124, but they had cleared it off again by 1962. They had a couple of bad years in the late 1970s, and their score went back to 100—exactly—for one moment (1977). By 1983 they had cleaned off their account again.

Beginning in 1989, however, the Tigers got themselves involved in some serious loss-related activity. They lost 103 games in 1989, and 109 games in 1995. In between they managed to have two winning seasons, but by 1998 they held the keys to the Port-a-Potty:

1998	Detroit	Tigers	AL	180
1998	Seattle	Mariners	AL	180
1998	Philadelphia	Phillies	NL	169
1998	Chicago	Cubs	NL	155
1998	Minnesota	Twins	AL	134

And they were just getting warmed up:

Year	City	Team	League	Won	Lost	Loser Score
1999	Detroit	Tigers	AL	69	92	209
2000	Detroit	Tigers	AL	79	83	220
2001	Detroit	Tigers	AL	66	96	258
2002	Detroit	Tigers	AL	55	106	318
2003	Detroit	Tigers	AL	43	119	404
2004	Detroit	Tigers	AL	72	90	433
2005	Detroit	Tigers	AL	71	91	465

The Tigers by 2005 were at a loser level not seen since 1969. This was not the first sign that baseball's era of competitive balance had come to an end, and it would not be the last:

2005	Detroit	Tigers	AL	465
2005	Pittsburgh	Pirates	NL	324
2005	Tampa Bay	Devil Rays	AL	293
2005	Kansas City	Royals	AL	282
2005	Milwaukee	Brewers	NL	274

After the Tigers' fine season in 2006, they were still the Big Losers, but the Pirates were ready to take over.

Pittsburgh Pirates

The Pirates, like the Tigers, are the heirs to a proud legacy. Ty Cobb; Honus Wagner. Al Kaline; Roberto Clemente. Mickey Lolich; Vern Law. Charlie Gehringer; Bill Mazeroski. Hank Greenberg; Willie Stargell.

The team now known as the Pirates began play in 1887, and they were Losers in their early years. They had a Loser Score of 152 in 1891, cleared that off by 1900, and never had a losing season again until 1914. A few subpar seasons then put them at 110 (1917), but they had cleared the books again by 1922. Between 1922 and 1945, the Pirates never had a Loser Score as high as 20.

Ralph Kiner joined the Pirates in 1946. I am not blaming Ralph Kiner for this, but the Ralph Kiner years were not good years for the Pirates. They lost 91 games in 1946, 96 games in 1950, 90 in 1951, 112 games in 1952, 104 games in 1953, 101 in 1954, 94 in 1955, and 92 in 1957. Their Loser Score peaked at 423 in 1957.

423 is a very significant Loser Score. That was a bad period. By 1959, however, the Pirates had cut their score to 292, and in 1960 they wiped it out by winning the World Series. For twenty years after that (up until 1984) the Pirates' Loser Score never reached as high as 20.

Some Pirates got caught up in the drug scandals of the 1980s, however, and by 1987 their Loser Score was up to 105. By 1992, they had wiped it out once more.

Theirs is a generally noble history. In one hundred plus years, the Pirates had had four periods of playing the Loser role, three of them brief, peaking in 1891, 1917 and 1987. They had had one period of very bad baseball, which we remember as the Ralph Kiner years. Beginning in 1993, however, the Pirates entered the dismal period in which they are still trapped. These are their won-lost records since 1993:

Year	Team	W	L	Loser Score
1993	Pirates	75	87	13
1994	Pirates	53	61	23
1995	Pirates	58	86	54
1996	Pirates	73	89	74
1997	Pirates	79	83	83
1998	Pirates	69	93	113
1999	Pirates	78	83	125
2000	Pirates	69	93	157
2001	Pirates	62	100	204
2002	Pirates	72	89	231
2003	Pirates	75	87	254
2004	Pirates	72	89	283
2005	Pirates	67	95	324
2006	Pirates	67	95	366
2007	Pirates	68	94	407
2008	Pirates	67	95	451
2009	Pirates	62	99	505
2010	Pirates	57	105	571

And these are the Biggest Losers in baseball, post 2010:

Year	City	Team	Lg	Loser Score
2010	Pittsburgh	Pirates	NL	571
2010	Kansas City	Royals	AL	441
2010	Baltimore	Orioles	AL	353
2010	Washington	Nationals	NL	258
2010	Detroit	Tigers	AL	219
2010	Milwaukee	Brewers	NL	198
2010	Tampa Bay	Rays	AL	145
2010	Cincinnati	Reds	NL	134
2010	Seattle	Mariners	AL	116
2010	Arizona	Diamondbacks	NL	101

Have we entered a new era of Big Losers?

Well…yes and no. The Pirates' Loser Score right now is the highest in baseball since 1969, but there were seven teams prior to 1969 that had higher scores.

The economic environment in baseball in the years 2000 to 2005 was very difficult for small city teams. Some franchises—Minnesota, St. Louis, Colorado—rose to that challenge. Some small-city franchises, most notably Pittsburgh and Kansas City, did not. They are the Big Losers in today's baseball. This, too, shall pass.

———··———

ADVERTISING

by Bill James

The essential problem of advertising—like all forms of propaganda—is that it requires increasingly large doses to get the same effect. I am referring here both to a narrow effect and a broad one. Let us suppose that there is a new product—new yummy zero-calories cherry goop—which must be introduced to the public by advertising. The first million spent in advertising the product will attract the most eager customers, those who are receptive to new products by nature, like cherry goop, and are in the habit of watching their calories. The second million moves down the chart to those who are less receptive to new products, like cherry goop less, and pay less attention to calories. The third million will be less effective than the second, and so on down the line. Eventually everybody who can tolerate cherry flavors has tried your product, and you can advertise until the cows come home and the Pirates win the pennant and it won't do any good.

That's the narrow effect, but there is also a broad effect: all advertising builds resistance to all advertising. We are all exposed to thousands of commercial messages every day now. We start to filter them out, having nothing to do with yummy cherry goop. The more commercials we see, the less attention we pay to each one, which requires the advertiser to be yet more active and more intrusive in trying to reach us.

We are living in the age not merely of advertising, but in the age of dead advertising; advertising no longer has much impact, so ever-larger doses of advertising are required to achieve ever-diminishing returns. There is an assumption, I think, that this will go on forever; that advertisers will become more and more clever about finding ways to invade our private spaces with their crap. I wonder. I wonder if it is possible that this whole thing will just...collapse.

In the e-universe people will review new products for their readers, and people who have new products to sell will reach people through those reviews, and everybody will realize that paying sports teams millions of dollars to name their stadiums after you and hanging banners everywhere is just a stupid waste of time and money.

It's a thought.

———

THIRTY-THREE ROTATIONS

by Bill James

**The 33 Greatest Starting Rotations of All-Time
In Chronological Order
Apropos of Nothing in Particular**

1. New York Giants, 1903.

First	Last	Lg	Year	G	IP	W	L	WPct	SO	BB	ERA
Joe	McGinnity	NL	1904	51	408.0	35	8	.814	144	86	1.61
Christy	Mathewson	NL	1904	48	367.2	33	12	.733	212	78	2.03
Luther	Taylor	NL	1904	37	296.1	21	15	.583	138	75	2.34
Hooks	Wiltse	NL	1904	24	164.2	13	3	.813	105	61	2.84

Joe McGinnity was named "The Iron Man" not because of his pitching load, but because his wife's family owned an Iron foundry in McAlester, Oklahoma. Pitching 408 innings and starting both games of double-headers and pitching in the minors until he was in his mid-fifties sort of kept the whole "Iron Man" thing going. Luther Taylor was a deaf mute who worked off-seasons for newspapers in two small towns in Kansas, Winchester and Oskaloosa. I used to live in Winchester, 90 years later, and had an office in Oskaloosa. Taylor was a likeable, friendly man who was a live wire despite his disability. Wiltse was called "Hooks" because of his curve ball.

2. Chicago White Sox, 1905.

First	Last	Lg	Year	G	IP	W	L	WPct	SO	BB	ERA
Nick	Altrock	AL	1905	38	316.0	23	12	.657	97	63	1.88
Frank	Owen	AL	1905	42	334.0	21	13	.618	125	56	2.10
Frank	Smith	AL	1905	39	291.2	19	13	.594	171	107	2.13
Doc	White	AL	1905	36	260.0	17	13	.567	120	58	1.77
Ed	Walsh	AL	1905	22	136.2	8	3	.727	71	29	2.17

Altrock was a guy with a funny-looking face who made a living as a comedian/coach for many years after his playing career. He did vaudeville in the off-season; during the season he was a legitimate coach, but he was a legitimate coach who doubled as an entertainer between innings and sometimes during innings. I'd like to see somebody do that now, and God knows there is no shortage of funny-looking coaches. Doc White held the record for consecutive scoreless innings for 60-some years, finally broken by Drysdale. Walsh, of course, is the big star of the group, but he didn't become a star until 1907.

3. Chicago Cubs, 1909.

First	Last	Lg	Year	G	IP	W	L	WPct	SO	BB	ERA
Three Finger	Brown	NL	1909	50	342.2	27	9	.750	172	53	1.31
Orval	Overall	NL	1909	38	285.0	20	11	.645	205	80	1.42
Ed	Reulbach	NL	1909	35	263.0	19	10	.655	105	82	1.78
Jack	Pfiester	NL	1909	29	197.0	17	6	.739	73	49	2.42
Rube	Kroh	NL	1909	17	120.1	9	4	.692	51	30	1.65

The Cubs had fantastic rotations every year in this era; I think 1909 was the best, and my rules don't allow multiple selections from the same team in the same decade. It wasn't really so much that these were great pitchers as it was that the infield behind them (Tinker, Evers and Chance) was so fantastic that they made whoever took the mound LOOK like a superstar in that game, with the dead balls and the infield grass four inches high.

4. Philadelphia Athletics, 1910.

First	Last	Lg	Year	G	IP	W	L	WPct	SO	BB	ERA
Jack	Coombs	AL	1910	45	353.0	31	9	.775	224	115	1.30
Chief	Bender	AL	1910	30	250.0	23	5	.821	155	47	1.58
Cy	Morgan	AL	1910	36	290.2	18	12	.600	134	117	1.55
Eddie	Plank	AL	1910	38	250.1	16	10	.615	123	55	2.01
Harry	Krause	AL	1910	16	112.1	6	6	.500	60	42	2.88

Bender and Plank were the Hall of Famers. This is actually the first team we've hit that won the World Series.

5. 1913 New York Giants.

First	Last	Lg	Year	G	IP	W	L	WPct	SO	BB	ERA
Christy	Mathewson	NL	1913	40	306.0	25	11	.694	93	21	2.06
Rube	Marquard	NL	1913	42	288.0	23	10	.697	151	49	2.50
Jeff	Tesreau	NL	1913	41	282.0	22	13	.629	167	119	2.17
Al	Demaree	NL	1913	31	200.0	13	4	.765	76	38	2.21

Mathewson and Marquard are Hall of Famers, although Marquard may be the worst pitcher in the Hall of Fame. Note that Demaree has only 17 decisions with 200 innings pitched—a sign that John McGraw by 1913 was already using his bullpen quite a bit.

6. 1917 Boston Red Sox.

First	Last	Lg	Year	G	IP	W	L	WPct	SO	BB	ERA
Babe	Ruth	AL	1917	41	326.0	24	13	.649	128	108	2.02
Carl	Mays	AL	1917	35	289.0	22	9	.710	91	74	1.74
Dutch	Leonard	AL	1917	37	294.0	16	17	.485	144	72	2.17
Ernie	Shore	AL	1917	29	227.0	13	10	.565	57	55	2.22
Rube	Foster	AL	1917	17	123.0	8	7	.533	34	53	2.56

Let me explain a little bit how I'm choosing these teams, because I'm choosing a lot of teams that didn't win the World Series or didn't even win their league, like the Red Sox, who won the World Series in 1916 and 1918, but not 1917. I'm choosing the teams in this way. First, I figure the Season Score for each pitcher. Then I multiply the Season Score for the #1 pitcher on the team by 1, for the number 2 pitcher by 2, for the number 3 pitcher by 3, and by the number 4 pitcher by 4. Then I'm choosing the three highest totals from each decade, except that I won't choose two teams from the same team in the same decade, and then I have some other little rules and stuff to handle hard cases.

7. 1920 Chicago White Sox.

First	Last	Lg	Year	G	IP	W	L	WPct	SO	BB	ERA
Red	Faber	AL	1920	40	319.0	23	13	.639	108	88	2.99
Eddie	Cicotte	AL	1920	37	303.0	21	10	.677	87	74	3.27
Dickie	Kerr	AL	1920	45	254.0	21	9	.700	72	72	3.37
Lefty	Williams	AL	1920	39	299.0	22	14	.611	128	90	3.91

The only team to have four twenty-game winners, other than the 1971 Orioles. Faber is in the Hall of Fame and Cicotte would be if he wasn't dirty, although actually Cicotte was a good guy who just got caught up in something he should have stayed away from. He was a very modest, very dignified man.

8. New York Giants, 1920.

First	Last	Lg	Year	G	IP	W	L	WPct	SO	BB	ERA
Fred	Toney	NL	1920	42	278.0	21	11	.656	81	57	2.65
Jesse	Barnes	NL	1920	43	293.0	20	15	.571	63	56	2.64
Art	Nehf	NL	1920	40	281.0	21	12	.636	79	45	3.07
Phil	Douglas	NL	1920	46	226.0	14	10	.583	71	55	2.71
Rube	Benton	NL	1920	33	193.0	9	16	.360	52	31	3.03

This is the first team we have hit that did not have a Hall of Famer in the starting rotation. These are all interesting guys. Toney was a big, strong guy who is famous for pitching half of the double no-hit game, matched up against Hippo Vaughn. He also was involved in a famous scandal in 1918 after he abandoned his wife and was living with some floozy. His wife sued him for non-support and he was prosecuted for violation of the Mann act (taking a woman across state lines for immoral purposes, probably involving sex,

I'm just guessing), and agreed to join the Army in exchange for the prosecution being dropped. Jesse Barnes was a cousin of mine, not really a distant cousin; his mother was a James, and he grew up about 20 miles from me. Art Nehf was a little lefty, sort of an earlier-day Carl Hubbell. Phil Douglas was thrown out of baseball after he wrote a spiteful letter, drunk, in which he sort of obliquely offered to throw games to get even with John McGraw for treating him so bad. Benton was an alcoholic who had a large number of incidents involving public intoxication, and bounced from team to team for that reason. He testified against the Black Sox before the grand jury investigating the 1919 fix, and was himself accused of making a lot of money betting against the Sox. Widely regarded as a ne'er-do-well and undesirable, he was released in mid-season 1921 although he was pitching well, and was banned from the American League by Ban Johnson, then re-instated by Commissioner Landis in direct contravention of Landis' announced policies, probably because Landis wanted to cut Ban Johnson off at the knees.

9. 1927 Yankees.

First	Last	Lg	Year	G	IP	W	L	WPct	SO	BB	ERA
Waite	Hoyt	AL	1927	36	256.0	22	7	.759	86	54	2.64
Wilcy	Moore	AL	1927	50	213.0	19	7	.731	75	59	2.28
Herb	Pennock	AL	1927	34	210.0	19	8	.704	51	48	3.00
Urban	Shocker	AL	1927	31	200.0	18	6	.750	35	41	2.84
Dutch	Ruether	AL	1927	27	184.0	13	6	.684	45	52	3.38
George	Pipgras	AL	1927	29	166.0	10	3	.769	81	77	4.12

Not as famous as the batting side of the team, but they're here on merit. Wilcy Moore was a reliever, but also made 12 starts and pitched 213 innings. Hoyt and Pennock are Hall of Famers, of course, although neither is overwhelmingly qualified, and Shocker, Ruether and Pipgras were all fine pitchers.

10. 1931 Philadelphia Athletics.

First	Last	Lg	Year	G	IP	W	L	WPct	SO	BB	ERA
Lefty	Grove	AL	1931	41	289.0	31	4	.886	175	62	2.06
George	Earnshaw	AL	1931	43	282.0	21	7	.750	152	75	3.67
Rube	Walberg	AL	1931	44	291.0	20	12	.625	106	109	3.74
Roy	Mahaffey	AL	1931	30	162.0	15	4	.789	59	82	4.22
Eddie	Rommel	AL	1931	25	118.0	7	5	.583	18	27	2.97

Lefty Grove was perhaps the greatest pitcher of all time, having his greatest season. Earnshaw for two or three years was a beast.

11. New York Giants, 1933.

First	Last	Lg	Year	G	IP	W	L	WPct	SO	BB	ERA
Carl	Hubbell	NL	1933	45	309.0	23	12	.657	156	47	1.66
Hal	Schumacher	NL	1933	35	259.0	19	12	.613	96	84	2.15
Freddie	Fitzsimmons	NL	1933	36	252.0	16	11	.593	65	72	2.89
Roy	Parmelee	NL	1933	32	218.0	13	8	.619	132	77	3.18

The Giants are hitting every decade—1903, 1913, 1920, 1933. They won the World Series in '33, and Hubbell was the MVP. Freddie Fitzsimmons was a fascinating guy, a squat man with unnaturally long arms, kind of a hobbit; nobody ever had much confidence in him but somehow he always won. Roy Parmalee was perhaps the hardest thrower in baseball at this time, and was always flirting with no-hitters. His fastball apparently had fantastic movement, leading to a lot of wild pitches and hit batsmen. There's a good entry on him in the Neyer/James Guide.

12. Chicago Cubs, 1935.

First	Last	Lg	Year	G	IP	W	L	WPct	SO	BB	ERA
Bill	Lee	NL	1935	39	252.0	20	6	.769	100	84	2.96
Lon	Warneke	NL	1935	42	262.0	20	13	.606	120	50	3.06
Larry	French	NL	1935	42	246.0	17	10	.630	90	44	2.96
Charlie	Root	NL	1935	38	201.0	15	8	.652	94	47	3.09
Roy	Henshaw	NL	1935	31	143.0	13	5	.722	53	68	3.27
Tex	Carleton	NL	1935	31	171.0	11	8	.579	84	60	3.89

The second team we have encountered without a Hall of Famer, although Warneke was very near to a Hall of Fame standard, Root won 201 games, and Big Bill Lee pitched at a Hall of Fame level from 1935 to 1939. The '35 Cubs might have won the World Series, but Charlie Grimm fantastically mis-handled his starting pitching, using Lee, Warneke and French all in one game, forcing him to start Tex Carleton, his sixth starter, the next day. It's one of the most obvious blunders in World Series history, but is hardly ever mentioned; Grimm escaped from it almost entirely unscathed.

13. Cincinnati Reds, 1940.

First	Last	Lg	Year	G	IP	W	L	WPct	SO	BB	ERA
Bucky	Walters	NL	1940	36	305.0	22	10	.688	115	92	2.48
Paul	Derringer	NL	1940	37	297.0	20	12	.625	115	48	3.06
Junior	Thompson	NL	1940	33	225.0	16	9	.640	103	96	3.32
Jim	Turner	NL	1940	24	187.0	14	7	.667	53	32	2.89
Whitey	Moore	NL	1940	25	117.0	8	8	.500	60	56	3.62

No Hall of Famers again, but they did win the World Series. Walters, the 1939 MVP, was fantastic again in 1940. Jim Turner and Bucky Walters were among the most prominent early pitching coaches.

14. St. Louis Cardinals, 1944.

First	Last	Lg	Year	G	IP	W	L	WPct	SO	BB	ERA
Mort	Cooper	NL	1944	34	252.0	22	7	.759	97	60	2.46
Ted	Wilks	NL	1944	36	208.0	17	4	.810	70	49	2.64
Harry	Brecheen	NL	1944	30	189.0	16	5	.762	88	46	2.86
Max	Lanier	NL	1944	33	224.0	17	12	.586	141	71	2.65
George	Munger	NL	1944	21	121.0	11	3	.786	55	41	1.34

The Cardinal farm system at this time was a machine, producing two to five outstanding pitching prospects every year, although oddly enough none of them became truly great. Cooper was the MVP in 1942, and pitched at a comparable level in '43 and '44. The 1944 Cardinals beat the Browns, who played in the same park, to win the World Championship. Lanier was banned from baseball for three years for signing with the Mexican League in '46; actually he was banned for life, but it was lifted after three years because he was able to prove that he had never associated with Pete Rose. His son was the shortstop from the 1960s—one of the worst hitting regulars of all time. By the early 1950s the entire National League was populated by Cardinal castoff pitchers.

15. Detroit Tigers, 1946.

First	Last	Lg	Year	G	IP	W	L	WPct	SO	BB	ERA
Hal	Newhouser	AL	1946	37	293.0	26	9	.743	275	98	1.94
Dizzy	Trout	AL	1946	38	276.0	17	13	.567	151	97	2.35
Virgil	Trucks	AL	1946	32	237.0	14	9	.609	161	75	3.23
Fred	Hutchinson	AL	1946	28	207.0	14	11	.560	138	66	3.09
Al	Benton	AL	1946	28	141.0	11	7	.611	60	58	3.64

Newhouser was at the level of Koufax, Carlton in '72, Guidry in '78. Trout and Trucks had wonderful arms and won 170 games apiece. Hutchinson, although most famous as a manager, was also notable for two other things: 1) he had the best control of his era, other than perhaps Robin Roberts, and 2) he was the best hitting pitcher of that generation, hitting .315 in 1946, .302 in '47, and .326 in 1950.

Hutchinson controlled the strike zone, both as a hitter and a pitcher, at a very unusual level. His strikeout/walk ratios, as a pitcher, were among the best of his era, if not the best of his era; he led the American League in strikeout/walk ratio four times. His strikeout/walk ratios, as a hitter, were perhaps the best of any pitcher since 1900.

16. New York Yankees, 1953.

First	Last	Lg	Year	G	IP	W	L	WPct	SO	BB	ERA
Ed	Lopat	AL	1953	25	178.0	16	4	.800	50	32	2.43
Whitey	Ford	AL	1953	32	207.0	18	6	.750	110	110	3.00
Johnny	Sain	AL	1953	40	189.0	14	7	.667	84	45	3.00
Vic	Raschi	AL	1953	28	181.0	13	6	.684	76	55	3.33
Allie	Reynolds	AL	1953	41	145.0	13	7	.650	86	61	3.41

The Yankees have rarely been known for outstanding starting pitching. It's one of those mind-numbingly obvious things that people will totally overlook when they are a'mind to lecture you about the importance of pitching; they'll talk about how it is great pitching that dominates in October, etc. etc., totally oblivious to the fact that the Yankees, who have had had several fairly good Octobers, have never really done it with pitching.

Casey, of course, switched his pitchers between starting and relief to get the matchups he wanted, in a way that would never be accepted now. In '53 he had five outstanding pitchers, all of whom had very good careers as well, but Sain and Reynolds relieved more often than they started, and the other guys relieved on occasion as well.

17. Cleveland Indians, 1954.

First	Last	Lg	Year	G	IP	W	L	WPct	SO	BB	ERA
Early	Wynn	AL	1954	40	271.0	23	11	.676	155	83	2.72
Bob	Lemon	AL	1954	36	258.0	23	7	.767	110	92	2.72
Mike	Garcia	AL	1954	45	259.0	19	8	.704	129	71	2.64
Art	Houtteman	AL	1954	32	188.0	15	7	.682	68	59	3.35
Bob	Feller	AL	1954	19	140.0	13	3	.813	59	39	3.09

This team is often cited as having the greatest starting rotation of all time, and it's certainly a legitimate candidate. 1954 was the right time to visit Cleveland, with Rock 'n Roll, the '54 Indians and the Sam Sheppard case. If we really listed the five best pitching rotations of the 1950s, I think that would be five Cleveland Indians teams…different combinations of Wynn, Lemon, Feller, Garcia, and Herb Score. In '54 Garcia led the league in ERA at 2.64—and their *team* ERA was 2.78.

This is the first rotation we have seen with *three* Hall of Famers, although you have to go to the #5 guy to reach the third Hall of Famer.

18. Chicago White Sox, 1954.

First	Last	Lg	Year	G	IP	W	L	WPct	SO	BB	ERA
Virgil	Trucks	AL	1954	40	265.0	19	12	.613	152	95	2.78
Sandy	Consuegra	AL	1954	39	154.0	16	3	.842	31	35	2.69
Bob	Keegan	AL	1954	31	210.0	16	9	.640	61	82	3.09
Jack	Harshman	AL	1954	35	177.0	14	8	.636	134	96	2.95
Don	Johnson	AL	1954	46	144.0	8	7	.533	68	43	3.13
Billy	Pierce	AL	1954	36	189.0	9	10	.474	148	86	3.48

1) The first team on the list without a Hall of Famer since the Cardinals in '44.
2) I think Virgil Trucks is the second pitcher to make our list twice, the other being Christy Mathewson.
3) This is a really interesting team. Trucks was a great pitcher with a fascinating career. Consuegra was a Cuban guy who made it to the majors late and didn't pitch a lot of innings, but pitched at an extremely high level of effectiveness from 1953 to 1955.

Harshman spent years trying to make the majors as a first baseman. He hit 37 homers in the minors in 1947, 40 homers in 1949, and 47 homers in 1951, but didn't get called up. He switched to pitching, made the majors in months, and had a good major league career, also hit 21 homers in 522 at bats in the majors. On August 13, 1954, he pitched a 16-inning shutout over Detroit, took one day off, and came in on August 15 to pitch two innings in relief.

Billy Pierce, of course, was a near-Hall of Famer who was outstanding in every season from 1951 to 1958 *except* 1954. Pierce also was a member of a rotation that could be listed here but isn't, the 1962 Giants, and pitched well enough in '62 to be one of four pitchers mentioned in the Cy Young voting that year.

19. New York Yankees, 1963.

First	Last	Lg	Year	G	IP	W	L	WPct	SO	BB	ERA
Whitey	Ford	AL	1963	38	269.0	24	7	.774	189	56	2.74
Jim	Bouton	AL	1963	40	249.0	21	7	.750	148	87	2.53
Ralph	Terry	AL	1963	40	268.0	17	15	.531	114	39	3.22
Al	Downing	AL	1963	24	176.0	13	5	.722	171	80	2.56
Stan	Williams	AL	1963	29	146.0	9	8	.529	98	57	3.21

This is a very underrated rotation, probably the best pitching rotation in the history of the New York Yankees, and, at least as it is scored by my system, the best pitching rotation of the 1960s.

Now that's a shocking thing for me to say, since I have always regarded the 1966 Dodgers as the greatest rotation of the 1960s, but this team scores better, and, now that I look at the facts, I kind of see the point. In number ones you've got Koufax against Ford. OK, maybe Koufax in '66 was better than Ford in '63, but Ford was awfully good. Ford had a longer career than Koufax, a better winning percentage, and a lower ERA, despite playing in a significantly higher run context.

OK, Ford in '63 wasn't Koufax in '66, but this isn't about the number ones; it's about the rotations. The '63 Yankees' #2, Jim Bouton, was better than anybody else the Dodgers had, and their #3, Ralph Terry, was a very good match for the Dodgers' #2, Osteen. Al Downing, a rookie who made 22 starts, was totally, Koufax-like dominant, posting the lowest hits/innings ratio in the majors in fourteen years, and Stan Williams was a more-than-competent #5.

20. The 1966 Dodgers.

First	Last	Lg	Year	G	IP	W	L	WPct	SO	BB	ERA
Sandy	Koufax	NL	1966	41	323.0	27	9	.750	317	77	1.73
Claude	Osteen	NL	1966	39	240.0	17	14	.548	137	65	2.85
Don	Sutton	NL	1966	37	225.2	12	12	.500	209	52	2.99
Don	Drysdale	NL	1966	40	274.0	13	16	.448	177	45	3.42

The starting rotation of the 1966 Dodgers has in the past, I am forced to conclude, been horribly overrated by...well, me. I have in the past listed this as one of the greatest starting rotations of all time. When I drew up this list they initially ranked sixth for the decade, which was a shock to me, and of course my first thought was to try to fix the system. But then I stopped to look at the facts.

The 1966 Dodgers have three Hall of Famers in their front four—one of the few teams ever that does—and the other starter won 196 games, so he wasn't chopped raisinettes, either. They pitched a ton of innings—1063 among the four of them—with good ERAs and good strikeout/walk ratios, and Koufax was one of the greatest ever. With a better offense behind them they might all have won 20 games, and Koufax might have won 30.

Yes, but. We all know that the low offense/great pitching thing is in large part a park illusion. The Dodger offense in '66, park-adjusted, was about average. Three of these guys have a combined won-lost record of 42-42, which, say what you will about won-lost records, is not all that good, and that's different in 84 decisions than it is in 27. If we adjust for the offensive support we have to adjust for the park as well. Drysdale's ERA was barely better than the league average if you don't park-adjust it, and, even pitching in the best pitcher's park in the league, no one on the team other than Koufax was anywhere near the league leaders in ERA.

It is a good staff, yes, but there are other staffs that have more to sell—better won-lost records, and better ERAs even if you don't park-adjust the ERAs. The three highest-scoring staffs of the 1960s, by the system I used here, are the '63 Yankees, the '68 Indians and the '69 Orioles. There are two problems with including the '69 Orioles: 1) that they are redundant of the 1971 Orioles, who will be included from the next decade, and 2) that we haven't included a National League pitching staff here since 1944, and we probably should find one that we like pretty soon.

OK, we throw out the Orioles, the Dodgers' are still fifth. They're fifth, but they rate a few points behind the '63 Cincinnati

Reds, and I couldn't really argue with a straight face that the '63 Reds had a better starting rotation than the '66 Dodgers (John Tsitouris, excuse me?). The other team they rate a few points behind is the '65 Dodgers, which is basically the same team, except that Drysdale was great in '65 and the fourth spot was occupied by an aging Johnny Podres, rather than a young Don Sutton.

Ultimately, I am happier with the '66 Dodgers on this list than without them, but I have to say, this is not the starting rotation that I have always thought that it was.

21. The 1968 Cleveland Indians.

First	Last	Lg	Year	G	IP	W	L	WPct	SO	BB	ERA
Luis	Tiant	AL	1968	34	258.1	21	9	.700	264	73	1.60
Sam	McDowell	AL	1968	38	269.0	15	14	.517	283	110	1.81
Stan	Williams	AL	1968	44	194.0	13	11	.542	147	51	2.51
Sonny	Siebert	AL	1968	31	206.0	12	10	.545	146	88	2.97

Second mention for Stan Williams. Two pitchers with 547 strikeouts between them and ERAs in the ones; that's pretty good. Third and fourth starters were winning pitchers with better-than-league ERAs in a neutral park, and they both had good careers.

Some people will be annoyed that none of the White Sox staffs with Gary Peters, Juan Pizarro, Tommy John and Joe Horlen made it on to the list, but that's just the way the scores worked out, and those teams received massive help from extremely low park factors.

22. The 1971 Baltimore Orioles.

First	Last	Lg	Year	G	IP	W	L	WPct	SO	BB	ERA
Jim	Palmer	AL	1971	37	282.0	20	9	.690	184	106	2.68
Pat	Dobson	AL	1971	38	282.0	20	8	.714	187	63	2.90
Dave	McNally	AL	1971	30	224.0	21	5	.808	91	58	2.89
Mike	Cuellar	AL	1971	38	292.0	20	9	.690	124	78	3.08

Four twenty-game winners. Cuellar and McNally were both as good as many pitchers who are in the Hall of Fame. The best starting rotation between the 1954 Indians and the 1990s Braves.

23. 1973 Los Angeles Dodgers.

First	Last	Lg	Year	G	IP	W	L	WPct	SO	BB	ERA
Don	Sutton	NL	1973	33	256.1	18	10	.643	200	56	2.42
Andy	Messersmith	NL	1973	33	250.0	14	10	.583	177	77	2.70
Tommy	John	NL	1973	36	218.0	16	7	.696	116	50	3.10
Claude	Osteen	NL	1973	33	237.0	16	11	.593	86	61	3.30
Al	Downing	NL	1973	30	193.0	9	9	.500	124	68	3.31

Second listing for Sutton, Osteen and Downing. All five legitimate high-quality pitchers, and perhaps the first team we've had with a true five-man rotation. I try to mention Andy Messersmith at BillJamesOnline.com at least once a week.

24. 1978 Kansas City Royals.

First	Last	Lg	Year	G	IP	W	L	WPct	SO	BB	ERA	Score
Larry	Gura	AL	1978	35	221.2	16	4	.800	81	60	2.72	249
Dennis	Leonard	AL	1978	40	294.2	21	17	.553	183	78	3.33	234
Paul	Splittorff	AL	1978	39	262.0	19	13	.594	76	60	3.40	207
Rich	Gale	AL	1978	31	192.1	14	8	.636	88	100	3.09	165

Funny; I would have expected the 1985 Royals to make the list for the 1980s—they weren't close—but would not have expected the '78 team to be here. All four of their starters had winning records and ERAs much better than the league, despite playing in a hitter's park.

Leonard won 20 games in '77, '78 and '80, and probably would have won 20 in 1981 were it not for the strike. Gale came out of the minors early in '78 and started 13-3. He was 6-foot-8 with a great, moving fastball, but he over-analyzed everything and was behind in the count from the day he was born. Splittorff still holds the Royals' record for career wins.

The interesting guy here was Larry Gura, who had been knocking around the majors for almost a decade before he finally nailed down a rotation spot with the '78 Royals, due to injuries to Steve Busby and Andy Hassler. Gura had come up with the Cubs under Durocher, and had bounced to the Yankees, where he went 5-1 with a 2.41 ERA in eight starts in 1974.

I would compare Gura very strongly to Craig Breslow, the

Yale-educated lefty who pitched in 75 games for Oakland in 2010; he's about the same size as Gura, same build, same coloring. Like Breslow, Gura was a lefty without an outstanding fastball, but like Breslow he was intelligent, had excellent balance and was always in shape. Breslow, like Gura, has struggled to get opportunities consistent with his performance.

After Gura went 5-1 with the Yankees in '74 the Yankees hired Billy Martin as their manager. Gura and Martin were like Marilyn Monroe and Curly from the Three Stooges; they just didn't really belong together. One time Martin saw Gura leaving the hotel in tennis whites. He might as well have been holding hands with Liberace. Not that Gura was gay; that's not what I'm saying. Martin was macho; worse, he was a midget, alcoholic macho who perpetually had to be more macho than the big guys. He was a moron; he was a great manager, but he was a troglodyte.

So anyway, Martin ran Gura out of New York, and Gura wound up in Kansas City, where he went 4-0 with a 2.30 ERA in 1976. Mid-1978, he was still struggling for starts. By mid-September he was 14-4 and still winning. I asked Whitey Herzog how he explained Gura's emergence. He looked at me straight and said, "It's just a man getting an opportunity and taking advantage of it."

I remember that I was so impressed by that answer, and I still am, because Herzog didn't try to dress up what had happened by talking about the great work of his pitching coach, or Gura's maturity, or how his slider had come around, or any of that nonsense. He frankly admitted, not in so many words, that Gura had always been able to pitch; he just hadn't given him the chance to do it before. Gura shut out Toronto late in the year; by now it seemed likely that the Royals would play the Yankees in October, but Billy Martin had been fired earlier in the season. Somebody asked Gura in the postgame scrum if it would mean more to him to play the Yankees if Billy Martin was still there.

"If Martin was still there," said Gura, "we'd be playing the Red Sox."

25. Dodgers, 1985.

First	Last	Lg	Year	G	IP	W	L	WPct	SO	BB	ERA
Orel	Hershiser	NL	1985	36	239.2	19	3	.864	157	68	2.03
Fernando	Valenzuela	NL	1985	35	272.1	17	10	.630	208	101	2.45
Bob	Welch	NL	1985	23	167.1	14	4	.778	96	35	2.31
Jerry	Reuss	NL	1985	34	212.2	14	10	.583	84	58	2.92
Rick	Honeycutt	NL	1985	31	142.0	8	12	.400	67	49	3.42

Which one of those guys wouldn't you want pitching for you? Jerry Reuss or Cole Hamels, who do you want? I'll take Reuss.

26. New York Mets, 1986.

First	Last	Lg	Year	G	IP	W	L	WPct	SO	BB	ERA
Bob	Ojeda	NL	1986	32	217.1	18	5	.783	148	52	2.57
Dwight	Gooden	NL	1986	33	250.0	17	6	.739	200	80	2.84
Ron	Darling	NL	1986	34	237.0	15	6	.714	184	81	2.81
Sid	Fernandez	NL	1986	32	204.1	16	6	.727	200	91	3.52
Rick	Aguilera	NL	1986	28	141.2	10	7	.588	104	36	3.88

By 1991 they were starting Wally Whitehurst, Anthony Young and Pete Schourek.

27. Oakland A's, 1989.

First	Last	Lg	Year	G	IP	W	L	WPct	SO	BB	ERA
Mike	Moore	AL	1989	35	241.2	19	11	.633	172	83	2.61
Dave	Stewart	AL	1989	36	257.2	21	9	.700	155	69	3.32
Bob	Welch	AL	1989	33	209.2	17	8	.680	137	78	3.00
Storm	Davis	AL	1989	31	169.1	19	7	.731	91	68	4.36

Second listing for Bob Welch. This team got 76 wins from their front four—probably the most in the last 30 years, I don't know—and three of those guys were really that good. They won the earthquake-delayed World Series over the Giants, but none of the starters will make the Hall of Fame. We haven't seen a Hall of Famer in one of these rotations since Sutton in '73.

28. Milwaukee Brewers, 1992.

First	Last	Lg	Year	G	IP	W	L	WPct	SO	BB	ERA
Chris	Bosio	AL	1992	33	231.1	16	6	.727	120	44	3.62
Jaime	Navarro	AL	1992	34	246.0	17	11	.607	100	64	3.33
Bill	Wegman	AL	1992	35	261.2	13	14	.481	127	55	3.20
Cal	Eldred	AL	1992	14	100.1	11	2	.846	62	23	1.79

This is the weakest starting rotation to make the list, and needless to say there are at least five Atlanta Braves' staffs from the 1990s that would rank ahead of it. With league ERAs around five, constantly juggling five-man rotations and the bullpens eating up more and more innings, it's hard to find starting rotations in the 1990s that put together four or five quality pitchers.

29. Chicago White Sox, 1993.

First	Last	Lg	Year	G	IP	W	L	WPct	SO	BB	ERA
Jack	McDowell	AL	1993	34	256.2	22	10	.688	158	69	3.37
Alex	Fernandez	AL	1993	34	247.1	18	9	.667	169	67	3.13
Wilson	Alvarez	AL	1993	31	207.2	15	8	.652	155	122	2.95
Jason	Bere	AL	1993	24	142.2	12	5	.706	129	81	3.47

I have less to say about the recent pitchers because I assume that everybody else remembers the same things I remember. I never know if this is a wise choice, or whether I should write to an unseen reader who doesn't remember that Black Jack McDowell was (and is) a rock musician as serious about his music as his pitching, or that he was one of the last pitchers to stubbornly burn himself out completing games he didn't need to complete, or that Wilson Alvarez threw a no-hitter in his second major league start, or that Alex Fernandez was once looked upon as the second coming of Tom Seaver. For the most part I assume that you know these things.

30. Atlanta Braves, 1997.

First	Last	Lg	Year	G	IP	W	L	WPct	SO	BB	ERA
Greg	Maddux	NL	1997	33	232.2	19	4	.826	177	20	2.20
Denny	Neagle	NL	1997	34	233.1	20	5	.800	172	49	2.97
John	Smoltz	NL	1997	35	256.0	15	12	.556	241	63	3.02
Tom	Glavine	NL	1997	33	240.0	14	7	.667	152	79	2.96

This, of course, is the greatest starting rotation of the last forty years, if not the greatest of all time. The Braves won 98 games and led the National League in ERA in 1992, the year before they signed Greg Maddux. I remember when Maddux signed there I thought that the the starting pitching could never live up to the expectations of their fans. They did.

31. Oakland A's, 2001.

First	Last	Lg	Year	G	IP	W	L	WPct	SO	BB	ERA
Mark	Mulder	AL	2001	34	229.1	21	8	.724	153	51	3.45
Tim	Hudson	AL	2001	35	235.0	18	9	.667	181	71	3.37
Barry	Zito	AL	2001	35	214.1	17	8	.680	205	80	3.49
Cory	Lidle	AL	2001	29	188.0	13	6	.684	118	47	3.59
Erik	Hiljus	AL	2001	16	66.0	5	0	1.000	67	21	3.41

Who has had a career like Barry Zito? Since 2001 (his first full season) he has never made less than 32 starts in a season. He has won 142 major league games, and he is 22 games over .500 in his career.

And yet, somehow, he is not only regarded as a failure, but as a symbol of failure, a symbol of the waste of money, and the waste of potential. Who else is like that?

Lidle is dead, of course. Tim Hudson, on the other hand, remains effective after all these years, or at least is effective again after his injury. Tim Hudson as of the end of the 2010 season had exactly the same career won-lost record as Sandy Koufax—165 wins, 87 losses.

32. Seattle Mariners, 2001.

First	Last	Lg	Year	G	IP	W	L	WPct	SO	BB	ERA
Freddy	Garcia	AL	2001	34	238.2	18	6	.750	163	69	3.05
Jamie	Moyer	AL	2001	33	209.2	20	6	.769	119	44	3.43
Aaron	Sele	AL	2001	34	215.0	15	5	.750	114	51	3.60
Paul	Abbott	AL	2001	28	163.0	17	4	.810	118	87	4.25
Joel	Pineiro	AL	2001	17	75.1	6	2	.750	56	21	2.03
John	Halama	AL	2001	31	110.1	10	7	.588	50	26	4.73

In 2001 and 2002 the Arizona Diamondbacks had perhaps the greatest one-two pitching punch in the history of baseball, Randy Johnson and Schilling, who were the two best pitchers in baseball both years, but they don't make the list because their fourth starter in 2001 was Brian Anderson (4-9, 5.20 ERA) and in 2002 it was Rick Helling (10-12, 4.51). Their number three starter both years, Miguel Batista, probably wasn't any better than John (Is Your Mama) Halama, the Mariners' number six. This list is more about depth on a starting pitching staff than the one-two punch at the top. Garcia and Jamie Moyer were a long way from Johnson and Schilling, but the D'Backs three-four guys were a longer way away from 32-9.

33. 2002 Atlanta Braves.

First	Last	Lg	Year	G	IP	W	L	WPct	SO	BB	ERA
Greg	Maddux	NL	2002	34	199.1	16	6	.727	118	45	2.62
Kevin	Millwood	NL	2002	35	217.0	18	8	.692	178	65	3.24
Tom	Glavine	NL	2002	36	224.2	18	11	.621	127	78	2.96
Damian	Moss	NL	2002	33	179.0	12	6	.667	111	89	3.42

2002, really? It seems like yesterday.

INCHES PER HOUR

by Bill James

—·—

I thought of this when I was fifteen years old, and have been puzzled by it ever since. Why is there not an accepted system to measure how hard it is raining?

The way this could be done is quite obvious. Visualize an instrument a little like a pinwheel, but instead of the fan blades of the pinwheel, four, six or eight "spokes" with a small, triangular paper or light plastic cup attached to each spoke, so that it catches the rain rather than catching the wind. There is a very, very low co-efficient of friction—like a pinwheel—so that as the rain falls in one cup the weight of the water drives that cup down, and more of the rain accumulates in the next cup on the wheel. As the wheel gathers momentum, each cup empties itself at the bottom and then is upside-down as it returns to the top, when it again begins to accumulate rainwater. As it rains harder the wheel will spin faster—thus, the speed at which the wheel spins measures how hard it is raining.

It seems to me that there is a clear and obvious need for a such a measurement…so much so that I always "hear the gap" where that measurement should be. I notice this, of course, because of baseball. The Red Sox had two rain delays on a Sunday in 2010, and the announcers tried to communicate how hard it was raining in the vague, imprecise language available to them: it is raining pretty hard; I don't think it is raining as hard now as it was a minute ago; it is coming down in buckets; if this rain keeps up we will have to stop the game; they can play through this type of rain; etc.

Wouldn't it be obviously better if they could communicate to us how hard it is actually raining? A "20" might mean that if it rained at this intensity for one hour that would result in two inches of rainfall.

Of course, it would take us a little while to learn the meaning of the terms, but if you grew up with a system like this, by the time you were an adult you would be able to just look at a rainstorm—even without a reading—and say "I'd guess we're at about 13 IPH right now", and

    a) the observer would be very nearly right almost all of the time, and

    b) the listener would know exactly what he meant.

IPH is Inches Per Hour; of course, it's not actually inches per hour, it's tenths of an inch per hour, but IPH sounds better than TPH. You'd know that, too, if you grew up with the system.

Over time, standards would evolve, records would develop, and the measurement would integrate itself into the weather vocabulary. It is now raining at 12 IPH in Poughkeepsie, 10 down in Spackenkill, 3 in Wappingers Falls, and now pouring down at 18 in Hyde Park. A 22 was reported an hour ago in Woodstock. Eventually a standard would develop to help determine when a baseball game should be stopped. Baseball games can be stopped for:

    a) lightning,

    b) wet grounds, or

    c) rain in excess of 15 IPH.

As long as you don't have lightning, as long as you don't have intolerably wet grounds, you can play baseball until you have a sustained rainfall of 15 IPH. You don't have managers complaining that the game should have been stopped; you don't have managers complaining the game shouldn't have been stopped. There's a standard. When the standard is met, the game is stopped.

Of course, you don't stop the game the moment that the scale touches 15; it would be a more complicated standard than that. You stop the game when the scale touches 20 or is sustained for two minutes at 15; something like that. You re-start the game when the rainfall drops below 5 IPH and stays there for ten minutes.

Over time, the existence of such a system would be useful in predicting rainfall patterns. Suppose that the metropolitan area is blanketed by a system of "rain meters" measuring how hard it is raining across the area. Over time, computer models would develop that could predict that, once it hits 7 IPH right here, it will hit 15 IPH one minute later. Then you don't have to wait until it hits 15 IPH; you can pull the players off the field and cover the field as soon as it becomes apparent that it very shortly WILL hit 15 IPH.

But it is very, very difficult to develop those computer models without an accurate measurement of exactly how hard it is raining at each location at each moment. It just seems obvious to me that such a system SHOULD exist, and I've always been puzzled by the fact that it doesn't.

THE EXPANSION TIME BOMB

by Bill James

———

Over the next thirty years, the *de facto* standards for induction into the Hall of Fame will change substantially. They will not change for the "worse", in the sense of changing downward. They will move upward. They have to. They will move upward by so much that it will put pressure on the Hall of Fame to revamp their election system, because players are being left out who not only meet but substantially exceed the historical standards for Hall of Fame selection. The Hall of Fame *will* revise and expand its selection processes to include more players—as they have revised their process many times in the past—but even so, "deserving" players (deserving in the sense of being better than those selected in the past) will continue to be excluded. The reason these things will happen is expansion.

Wait a minute (I hear you saying); expansion began in 1961. There hasn't been an expansion now for more than ten years. Why is this an issue now? But the effects of expansion on Hall of Fame election are not felt *at all* for about 25 years after the first expansion, and are but slightly felt at first after that.

What we are really talking about here is the ratio of accomplishments by eligible players to Hall of Fame selections. That ratio, having begun to increase sometime in the mid-1980s, then increased a tiny bit more, and a tiny bit more, and a tiny bit more, like interest compounding at some low percentage. As a consequence of these small movements and as a consequence of other events, a point was reached about 2002 where there was a significant impact. That impact grows larger now every year, and will continue to do so for many years into the future. Eventually, it will dramatically alter the Hall of Fame discussion. This hasn't happened yet, but it will happen. The goal of this article is to open your eyes to it, so that when it happens you will be in a better position to understand the debate.

We are going to need a bunch of timelines in this article. Major league baseball began in 1876, let us say; some people prefer 1871 and reason prefers 1901, but my data sources are organized around 1876, so let's stick with that. The cumulative number of major league teams there have ever been, beginning in 1876, was as follows:

Year	Teams	Year	Teams	Year	Teams	Year	Teams	Year	Teams
		1880	36	1980	213	1900	334	1910	494
		1881	44	1891	230	1901	350	1911	510
		1882	58	1892	242	1902	366	1912	526
		1883	74	1893	254	1903	382	1913	542
		1884	108	1894	266	1904	398	1914	566
		1885	124	1895	278	1905	414	1915	590
1876	8	1886	140	1896	290	1906	430	1916	606
1877	14	1887	156	1897	302	1907	446	1917	622
1878	20	1888	172	1898	314	1908	462	1918	638
1879	28	1889	188	1899	326	1909	478	1919	654

By 1919 there had been 654 major league team/seasons, as we have decided to count them. This would double before expansion:

Year	Teams	Year	Teams	Year	Teams	Year	Teams	Year	Teams
1920	670	1930	830	1940	990	1950	1150	1960	1310
1921	686	1931	846	1941	1006	1951	1166		
1922	702	1932	862	1942	1022	1952	1182		
1923	718	1933	878	1943	1038	1953	1198		
1924	734	1934	894	1944	1054	1954	1214		
1925	750	1935	910	1945	1070	1955	1230		
1926	766	1936	926	1946	1086	1956	1246		
1927	782	1937	942	1947	1102	1957	1262		
1928	798	1938	958	1948	1118	1958	1278		
1929	814	1939	974	1949	1134	1959	1294		

And it has essentially doubled again since expansion:

Year	Teams	Year	Teams	Year	Teams	Year	Teams	Year	Teams
1960	1310	1970	1516	1980	1764	1990	2024	2000	2306
1961	1328	1971	1540	1981	1790	1991	2050	2001	2336
1962	1348	1972	1564	1982	1816	1992	2076	2002	2366
1963	1368	1973	1588	1983	1842	1993	2104	2003	2396
1964	1388	1974	1612	1984	1868	1994	2132	2004	2426
1965	1408	1975	1636	1985	1894	1995	2160	2005	2456
1966	1428	1976	1660	1986	1920	1996	2188	2006	2486
1967	1448	1977	1686	1987	1946	1997	2216	2007	2516
1968	1468	1978	1712	1988	1972	1998	2246	2008	2546
1969	1492	1979	1738	1989	1998	1999	2276	2009	2576

I became a baseball fan in 1961. Essentially one-half of all the major league teams there have ever been have played since I became I fan.

What is relevant is not the number of team/seasons, exactly, but the number of Hall of Fame type accomplishments. What are "Hall of Fame type accomplishments"? Well, you know…hitting .300, scoring 100 runs, driving in 100 runs, getting 200 hits, leading the league in something significant, winning 20 games, throwing a no-hitter, getting 200 strikeouts, winning an Award, playing in an All-Star game, getting a big hit in a World Series game. Those kind of things; there are Hall of Fame type accomplishments for a season, and there are Hall of Fame type accomplishments for a career. As there are more teams, there are more players having Hall of Fame type accomplishments.

Let us say, as a working assumption, that there are five Hall of Fame type accomplishments for each team. That may seem a little high intuitively, but it isn't; it's actually low. Look up a few teams. Almost every team has at least a couple of guys meeting one standard or another, and some teams have 20+ Hall of Fame accomplishments on the roster. It doesn't actually matter for our present analysis what the number is; let's just say it is five per team.

So by 1935, as there had been 910 teams, there had been four to five thousand Hall of Fame type accomplishments. Of course, through 1935 there had been no players selected to the Hall of Fame, since the Hall of Fame prior to 1935 was merely an abstract idea. Selections began in 1936, with 5 players. There were 7 more persons selected in 1937, 3 in 1938, and 10 in 1939:

Year	Teams	Hall of Fame Type Accomplishments	Running Total
1935	910	4550	0
1936	926	4630	5
1937	942	4710	10
1938	958	4790	11
1939	974	4870	21

Got ya, din' I? With 5, 7, 3 and 10, that would be a total of 25 by 1939, not 21. It's only 21, however, because the first 25 included Morgan Bulkeley, Ban Johnson, Alexander Cartwright and Henry Chadwick, none of whom ever played in the majors; they were selected for other contributions to the game.

It is not always clear who should "count" in this way. We could count only those who were selected as major league players, but there are also many people who were very, very good players, but who were selected as managers or in some other role—Clark Griffith, for example, won 237 games with a very good winning percentage, but was selected for his role as a team owner, and John McGraw, who had one of the highest on base percentages of all time, was selected as a manager.

The key to our analysis here is the relationship between on-field accomplishments in the organized major leagues, and Hall of Fame selections. As such, we're going to focus on the number of persons selected *who had played in the major leagues*—the white major leagues. As the Negro League players are perforce excluded from our count of teams, they must also be excluded from the count of accomplishments. But if you played in the majors at all, you're included in the count. Walter Alston had one major league at bat and struck out, but he played in the major leagues, so he counts. Willard Brown counts.

OK, by 1939 there were 21 players who had played in the major leagues, and who had been selected to the Hall of Fame. There had been almost 5,000 Hall of Fame type accomplishments. That's one Hall of Famer for every 230+ Hall of Fame type accomplishments.

Except that this assumes that the Hall of Fame is electing people now based on what they did yesterday. In reality, the Hall of Fame has always made most of its selections based on what players did 30, 40, and 50 years ago. The accomplishments of players

25 years ago are, as of yet, but lightly honored. Go back 25 years ago, and look at the star players: Jack Morris, Don Mattingly, Dale Murphy, Tim Raines, Fred Lynn, Ron Guidry, Barry Larkin. Many of these players eventually will be in the Hall of Fame; they're just not there yet. The accomplishments of the 1980s have not yet been fully honored by the Hall.

If you look forward to 1990, the accomplishments of the stars of 1990 have barely begun to poke into the Hall of Fame. By 1990 the major leagues included Griffey, Bonds, McGwire, Clemens, Maddux, Smoltz, Schilling. Even if you look back to 1980 or 1970, there are still many stars who will later be honored by the Hall of Fame, but have not yet been.

What I am saying is that there is a lag time between the "pile of gross accomplishments" and the granting of honors based on those accomplishments. Look at it this way: the last twelve men elected to the Hall of Fame who played major league baseball were Bert Blyleven, Roberto Alomar, Andre Dawson, Jim Rice, Whitey Herzog, Rickey Henderson, Joe Gordon, Dick Williams, Billy South-worth, Goose Gossage, Cal Ripken, Tony Gwynn. At least 90% of the accomplishments which put those men in the Hall of Fame were more than 20 years ago; at least 70% of them were more than 25 years ago. There is a lag time between accomplishment and honor, which we will say is 25 years.

This lag time was originally larger than it is now. When the Hall of Fame opened its doors it was 60 years behind in its work, and it took it about 40 years to catch up. Players elected in the 1940s included Rube Waddell, Jimmy Collins, Joe Tinker, Frank Chance, Eddie Plank, Fred Clarke, Ed Walsh and Ed Delahanty, all of them stars of the 1900-1910 era—and included many from before then, many from the 19th century. The Hall of Fame started out about 60 years behind in its honoring, and closed the margin gradually until they were only (let us say) about 25 years behind.

So the relevant number to represent the size of the pile of accomplishments in 1940 isn't based on the number of teams up to 1940, but on the number of teams up to 1915. By 1915 there had been 590 major league teams, so there had been, let us say, 2950 Hall of Fame type accomplishments. By 1940 there had been 21 major league players elected to the Hall of Fame.

Let us say that each Hall of Fame selection clears off 40 Hall of Fame type accomplishments. By 1940, then, the Hall of Fame was about 2,110 accomplishments behind in its work—2,950, minus 21 * 40. By 1950, as the Hall of Fame elected 32 players during the 1940s, this number had been reduced to 1,630:

Year	Inductees	Accomplishments Cleared	Honored Through Years	Teams Through That Year	Accomplishments Through That Team	Deficit
1940	**21**	**840**	**1915**	**590**	**2950**	**2110**
1941	22	840	1916	606	3030	2190
1942	22	880	1917	622	3110	2330
1943	22	880	1918	638	3190	2310
1944	22	880	1919	654	3270	2390
1945	33	1320	1920	670	3350	2030
1946	44	1760	1921	686	3430	1670
1947	48	1920	1922	702	3510	1590
1948	50	2000	1923	718	3590	1590
1949	53	2120	1924	734	3670	1550
1950	**53**	**2120**	**1925**	**750**	**3750**	**1630**

I have been doing a lot of "let us say" math here, but the exact numbers aren't the point. Whether you say there are five Hall of Fame Accomplishments per team per season or eight, whether you say that each selection clears 40 Accomplishments off the deck or 60, whether you say the lag time is 25 years or 35, it doesn't really matter. The math in these charts is going to work out about the same anyway; I'm just trying to use reasonable numbers to illustrate the point. I'm not claiming it IS 5.00 accomplishments per team or anything like that.

The honoring process was relatively slow throughout the 1950s, but by 1960—about the time I became a baseball fan—the Hall of Fame had cut the deficit to 1550 honors:

Year	Inductees	Accomplishments Cleared	Honored Through Years	Teams Through That Year	Accomplishments Through That Team	Deficit
1950	**53**	**2120**	**1925**	**750**	**3750**	**1630**
1951	55	2200	1926	766	3830	1630
1952	57	2280	1927	782	3910	1630
1953	62	2480	1928	798	3990	1510
1954	65	2600	1929	814	4070	1470
1955	71	2840	1930	830	4150	1310
1956	73	2920	1931	846	4230	1310
1957	74	2960	1932	862	4310	1350
1958	74	2960	1933	878	4390	1430
1959	75	3000	1934	894	4470	1470
1960	**75**	**3000**	**1935**	**910**	**4550**	**1550**

With some more aggressive honorin' in the 1960s, they had reduced that by 1970 to 1,110:

Year	Inductees	Accomplishments Cleared	Honored Through Years	Teams Through That Year	Accomplishments Through That Team	Deficit
1960	**75**	**3000**	**1935**	**910**	**4550**	**1550**
1961	77	3080	1936	926	4630	1550
1962	81	3240	1937	942	4710	1470
1963	85	3400	1938	958	4790	1390
1964	92	3680	1939	974	4870	1190
1965	92	3680	1940	990	4950	1270
1966	94	3760	1941	1006	5030	1270
1967	97	3880	1942	1022	5110	1230
1968	99	3960	1943	1038	5190	1230
1969	103	4120	1944	1054	5270	1150
1970	**106**	**4240**	**1945**	**1070**	**5350**	**1110**

And, with the help of Frankie Frisch and his madcap cronies, by 1985 they had entirely wiped out the backlog:

Year	Inductees	Accomplishments Cleared	Honored Through Years	Teams Through That Year	Accomplishments Through That Team	Deficit
1970	**106**	**4240**	**1945**	**1070**	**5350**	**1110**
1971	113	4520	1946	1086	5430	910
1972	118	4720	1947	1102	5510	790
1973	123	4920	1948	1118	5590	670
1974	128	5120	1949	1134	5670	550
1975	132	5280	1950	1150	5750	470
1976	136	5440	1951	1166	5830	390
1977	140	5600	1952	1182	5910	310
1978	142	5680	1953	1198	5990	310
1979	144	5760	1954	1214	6070	310
1980	147	5880	1955	1230	6150	270
1981	149	5960	1956	1246	6230	270
1982	152	6080	1957	1262	6310	230
1983	156	6240	1958	1278	6390	150
1984	161	6440	1959	1294	6470	30
1985	**165**	**6600**	**1960**	**1310**	**6550**	**-50**

I know when Frankie Frisch died; don't write me letters. I am using Frankie to stand in for that entire generation of voters, who selected 59 former players between 1970 and 1985. Twenty-four were selected by the BBWAA; 35 by other selectors.

Anyway, 1985 is 24 years after the first expansion. The expansion effects are just now beginning to show. Over the next 17 years, the ratio of accomplishments to honorees stayed about constant, and the deficit near zero:

Year	Inductees	Accomplishments Cleared	Honored Through Years	Teams Through That Year	Accomplishments Through That Team	Deficit
1985	**165**	**6600**	**1960**	**1310**	**6550**	**-50**
1986	168	6720	1961	1328	6640	-80
1987	170	6800	1962	1348	6740	-60
1988	171	6840	1963	1368	6840	0
1989	174	6960	1964	1388	6940	-20
1990	176	7040	1965	1408	7040	0
1991	180	7200	1966	1428	7140	-60
1992	183	7320	1967	1448	7240	-80
1993	184	7360	1968	1468	7340	-20
1994	187	7480	1969	1492	7460	-20
1995	190	7600	1970	1516	7580	-20
1996	191	7640	1971	1540	7700	60
1997	194	7760	1972	1564	7820	60
1998	194	7880	1973	1588	7940	60
1999	201	8040	1974	1612	8060	20
2000	205	8200	1975	1636	8180	-20
2001	**208**	**8320**	**1976**	**1660**	**8300**	**-20**

You see my point? About 1985, we finally reached a "stable point" in the Hall of Fame process, in which the old debts had been paid off, and the Hall was up to date on its work. That's where we stayed, and that's where we have been during most of my career—most of your adult lives, I would guess, for many of you.

About that time the Hall of Fame changed the Veterans' Committee process, which is unnecessary to say; the Hall of Fame changes the Veterans' Committee process all of the time, so one could say about *any* year that about that year the Hall of Fame changed the Veterans' Committee process. It's always true. Anyway, for several years the Veterans stopped selecting anybody. This threw off the balance:

Year	Inductees	Accomplishments Cleared	Honored Through Years	Teams Through That Year	Accomplishments Through That Team	Deficit
2001	**208**	**8320**	**1976**	**1660**	**8300**	**-20**
2002	209	8360	1977	1686	8430	70
2003	211	8440	1978	1712	8560	120
2004	213	8520	1979	1738	8690	170
2005	215	8600	1980	1764	8820	220
2006	217	8680	1981	1790	8950	270
2007	219	8760	1982	1816	9080	320
2008	223	8920	1983	1842	9210	290
2009	226	9040	1984	1868	9340	300
2010	**228**	**9120**	**1985**	**1894**	**9470**	**350**

The ratio of Hall of Fame type accomplishments to Hall of Fame selections has substantially increased in the last ten years. What does that mean? That means it's substantially more difficult to get into the Hall of Fame than it was ten years ago.

"Good!" you may be saying. "It's about god-damned time for that." I'm not arguing with you. I'm not arguing pro; I'm not arguing con. I am pointing this out—1) That there has been a shift in the ratio of Hall of Fame type accomplishments to Hall of Fame selections, and 2) That this change is nothing compared to the change that is going to occur if we continue along the course we are now marching.

From 1961 to 1970 there were 31 ex-players selected to the Hall of Fame. From 1971 to 1980 there were 41; from 1981 to 1990, 29; from 1991 to 2000, 29; and from 2001 through 2010, 23. Let us say that we elect 25 men to the Hall of Fame in the next ten years, and 25 in the ten years after that. What is this chart going to look like, then, in 2030?

Year	Inductees	Accomplishments Cleared	Honored Through Years	Teams Through That Year	Accomplishments Through That Team	Deficit
2010	**228**	**9120**	**1985**	**1894**	**9470**	**350**
2011	230	9200	1986	1920	9600	400
2012	233	9320	1987	1946	9730	410
2013	235	9400	1988	1972	9860	460
2014	238	9520	1989	1998	9990	470
2015	240	9600	1990	2024	10120	520
2016	243	9720	1991	2050	10250	530
2017	245	9800	1992	2076	10380	580
2018	248	9920	1993	2104	10520	600
2019	250	10000	1994	2132	10660	660
2020	253	10120	1995	2160	10800	680
2021	255	10200	1996	2188	10940	740
2022	258	10320	1997	2216	11080	760
2023	260	10400	1998	2246	11230	830
2024	263	10520	1999	2276	11380	860
2025	265	10600	2000	2306	11530	930
2026	268	10720	2001	2336	11680	960
2027	270	10800	2002	2366	11830	1030
2028	273	10920	2003	2396	11980	1060
2029	275	11000	2004	2426	12130	1130
2030	**278**	**11120**	**2005**	**2456**	**11280**	**1160**

And ten years after that, it will look like this:

Year	Inductees	Accomplishments Cleared	Honored Through Years	Teams Through That Year	Accomplishments Through That Team	Deficit
2040	**303**	**12120**	**2015**	**2756**	**13780**	**1660**

Over the next twenty to thirty years, if we continue to elect Hall of Famers at something like the pace of the last fifteen to twenty years, there will begin to develop a huge backlog of players who have not been selected, despite accomplishments greater than those who were honored in the years 1980 to 2005, when the ratio of accomplishments to honorees was historically stable. What that will mean is that players who have accomplishments like those of Goose Gossage, Kirby Puckett, Bill Mazeroski and Tony Perez will not be honored—players like that, and some better than that.

Of course, this argument is entangled with every other Hall of Fame argument. The perceptiveness and consistency of the voters is an issue. Ross Youngs and George Kell were not better players than Ken Boyer and Ron Santo; they just weren't. There's really no way to argue that they were.

In the 1940s, the Hall of Fame selected a whole bunch of people who maybe weren't *exactly* great ballplayers. This tied the Hall of Fame argument into a knot, and that knot can never be untied. The only way to make the Hall of Fame "fair" and "consistent" would be to honor everybody in baseball history as good as or better than Rico Petrocelli, and we are not going to do that. Since we are not going to do that, there are always going to be inequities in who is selected.

There is also generational inequity. There are some time periods in baseball history that have been treated kindly by the voters; there are others, not so much. I'm not getting into that; I'm not dealing with that here. I'm just trying to get you to understand a dimension to the issue that, up to now, I don't think very many people understand.

———·———

SHAKESPEARE AND VERLANDER

by Bill James

———

PART I—SHAKESPEARE

The population of Topeka, Kansas, today is roughly the same as the population of London in the time of Shakespeare, and the population of Kansas now is roughly the same as the population of England at that time. London at the time of Shakespeare had not only Shakespeare—whoever he was—but also Christopher Marlowe, Francis Bacon, Ben Jonson, and various other men of letters who are still read today. I doubt that Topeka today has quite the same collection of distinguished writers.

Why is this?

There are two theories that present themselves. One is that the talent that assembled in Shakespeare's London was a random cluster, an act of God to locate in this one place and time a very unusual pile of literary talent. The other theory is that there is talent everywhere; it is merely that some societies are good at developing it and other societies not so good.

You may choose which side of this argument you wish to squat upon, but I am on the (b) side; it is my very strong belief that there is talent everywhere and all the time, but that London at that time was very, very good at calling out the literary talent of its citizenry, whereas most places and most times are not nearly so effective along this line. I believe that there is a Shakespeare in Topeka, Kansas, today, that there is a Ben Jonson, that there is a Marlowe and a Bacon, most likely, but that we are unlikely ever to know who these people are because our society does not encourage excellence in literature. That's my opinion.

This observation is nowhere near as gloomy as it might seem. Our society is very, very good at developing certain types of skills and certain types of genius. We are fantastically good at identifying and developing athletic skills—better than we are, really, at almost anything else. We are quite good at developing and rewarding inventiveness. We are pretty good at developing the skills necessary to run a small business—a fast-food restaurant, for example. We're really, really good at teaching people how to drive automobiles and how to find a coffee shop.

We are not so good at developing great writers, it is true, but why is this? It is simply because we don't need them. We still have Shakespeare. We still have Thomas Hardy and Charles Dickens and Robert Louis Stevenson; their books are still around. We don't genuinely need more literary geniuses. One can only read so many books in a lifetime. We need new athletes all the time because we need new games every day—fudging just a little on the definition of the word "need". We like to have new games every day, and, if we are to have a constant and endless flow of games, we need a constant flow of athletes. We have gotten to be very, very good at developing the same.

There are people who believe that when baseball leagues expand, this leads inevitably to a decline in the quality of talent. In my view, this is preposterous. Talent—like stupidity—lies all around us in great heaps: talent that is undeveloped because of a shortage of opportunity, talent that is undeveloped because of laziness and inertia, talent that is undeveloped because there is no genuine need for it. When baseball leagues expand, that simply creates a need for more talent, which creates more opportunity, which—in a society like ours, which is brilliant at developing athletic ability—leads in very quick order to the development of more players.

Baseball *could* expand so rapidly that it outpaces the available latent talent, true—if it expanded too rapidly, or if it expanded to, let us say, 5,000 major league teams. There probably is not enough talent to stock 5,000 major league teams in a place the size of North America without some small slippage in ability, even if the transition from 30 teams to 5,000 was carefully managed. If we went from 30 teams to a mere 300, on the other hand, carefully managing the expansion, it would make no difference whatsoever in the quality of talent. That's my view.

PART II—VERLANDER
Justin Verlander of the Detroit Tigers is a magnificent pitcher. Watching him pitch one afternoon last year against Clay Buchholz, I was struck by how many outstanding young pitchers there are in baseball today. Jon Lester of the Red Sox is a tremendous pitcher. Is he *better* than Greinke or Lincecum or Felix Hernandez or David Price or Ubaldo Jimenez? Well, no—but he's just as good.

I have been a baseball fan for 50 years, and I have never seen the game so flush with tremendous young pitchers. We had a fling of great pitchers in the 1960s, yes, and another very impressive collection of pitchers in the mid-1970s: Seaver and Palmer and Catfish Hunter and Steve Carlton and Nolan Ryan and all those guys. But I've never seen the depth of quality young pitching that we have now.

So is it a random cluster, or is it a rational response to need?

It's a random cluster…or, at least, I think it is.

You can't make rules for the Almighty. Suppose that you create 100 great young pitchers, and you sprinkle them randomly across history. Will you get one coming along every year or two, or will you get clusters?

Obviously, you'll get clusters. After Seaver and Palmer and Catfish Hunter and Carlton there were no outstanding young pitchers in the major leagues for ten years, then there was another wave of them, Clemens and Saberhagen and Dwight Gooden and David Cone and others. We're at the crest now of another wave—the biggest wave of my lifetime, I believe.

PART III—TECHNICAL DETOUR

I was thinking, while watching Verlander work, that there is something very unusual here, which is this. When Verlander was a rookie in 2006, he won 17 games, but he struck out only 124 batters. In 2010 he struck out 269 batters. That's got to be very unusual, right, to have that kind of an increase in strikeouts *after having been successful without strikeouts*?

When Verlander was a rookie he just basically threw fastballs. He threw 100 MPH fastballs, so this was effective, and he had a changeup and a curve, which basically he could get by with throwing because his fastball was so good. Now, his curve is outstanding and he cuts the fastball sometimes so that it, too, has become a strikeout pitch. It is unusual to see a pitcher improve that much after he is already successful. The normal pattern is that when a player is successful, he continues to do what he is doing until it is no longer successful.

So, I identified all pitchers in history who

a) were rookies,
b) pitched 140 or more innings, and
c) had strikeout rates below the league norm.

There were 600 such pitchers—an even 600, which we could call the Verlander group, except that to form a true Verlander group, we would need a fourth criterion: that the pitcher was successful as a rookie.

Anyway, Verlander last year was +86 strikeouts—that is, 86 strikeouts more than an average American League pitcher in the same number of innings. What I was wondering was, has there ever before been a pitcher who started out *below* average in strikeouts, and then had a season in which he was almost 100 strikeouts *above* average?

Hardie Henderson was below the league average in strikeouts as a rookie in 1883 and then, in 1884, struck out 346 batters in 439 innings, which was 208 strikeouts above average. This, however, was 1884, and 1884 doesn't really count. Two things happened in 1884 which make it peculiar. First, there was an extremely rapid expansion of immature leagues, which caused a precipitous drop in the quality of talent. Second, 1884 was the season in which baseball more or less abandoned its efforts to enforce the rule that pitchers were required to throw underhanded. There was a rapid switch from throwing underhanded to throwing overhand. Thus, when we draw up a list of the largest "+ strikeout seasons" by pitchers who began their careers with below-average strikeout rates, the top nine pitchers on the list are from 1884, 1884, 1884, 1884, 1883, 1884, 1885, 1932 and 1884.

Nineteenth century baseball has few of the characteristics of major league baseball so let's drop the 19th century pitchers from the list. When we drop the 19th century pitchers from the list, we get the following list of "plus strikeout seasons" by pitchers who had below-average strikeout rates as rookies (with "K Adv" being the number of strikeouts they had that year above the league average for pitchers that year):

First	Last	Team	Lg	Year	K Adv
Red	Ruffing	New York Yankees	AL	1932	96
Ben	Sheets	Milwaukee Brewers	NL	2004	87
Justin	Verlander	Tigers	AL	2009	86
Clay	Kirby	San Diego Padres	NL	1971	70
Zack	Greinke	Royals	AL	2009	67
Rick	Sutcliffe	Indians-Cubs	NL	1984	65
Bump	Hadley	Washington Senators	AL	1930	65
Kevin	Brown	San Diego Padres	NL	1998	63
Cy	Young	Boston Red Sox	AL	1905	61
Jim	Lonborg	Boston Red Sox	AL	1967	60

One can argue that Verlander is unique, however, because he was successful as a rookie. Ruffing as a rookie was 9-18, the following year 6-15, the following year 5-13. One can understand that a pitcher of that quality would tinker with his stuff, trying to learn new pitches. Ben Sheets as a rookie was 11-10, but with a 4.76 ERA, and, in his next season, 11-16 with a 4.15. Naturally he would try some other pitches.

The closest parallel to Verlander, actually, is Rick Sutcliffe. As a rookie in 1979 Sutcliffe was 17-10 with a 3.46 ERA, 117 strikeouts—very similar to Verlander. After that season he had some injuries and also some very serious conflicts with his manager, Tommy Lasorda, and got traded a couple of times before re-emerging as a quality pitcher. But Sutcliffe might be more like Greinke than Verlander.

Clay Kirby, who was a real hard thrower like Verlander, was 7-20 as a rookie although he had a good ERA. He increased his strikeouts in two years from 113 to 231 and was a good pitcher, although he always had some control issues.

Verlander just started out good and then got better, which is pretty unique, but then everybody is unique in one way or another, I guess. Other pitchers who started out with low K rates and then had big strikeout increases include Darryl Kile, Esteban Loaiza, Daniel Cabrera, Ricky Nolasco and Jeremy Bonderman.

There clearly are far more of these pitchers in recent years than in any other period in baseball history, which may be trying to tell us something about how pitchers are developed now. Pitchers in the 1930s/1940s were expected to be able to throw every pitch by the time they got to the majors, and also were expected to be able to drop down and throw sidearm. That was one extreme; we may be at the other end now. Now, if a pitcher throws really hard, we don't want him to try to do too much in the minor leagues. Just gain command of the delivery and a couple of pitches to keep the hitter from sitting on your fastball, then we'll bring you to the majors and you can expand your repertoire once you're established there.

A couple of incidental things I learned while doing this study.

First, Kirk Rueter in 2004 struck out 56 batters in 190.1 innings. The National League norm in 2004 was 6.74 strikeouts per nine innings, so Rueter was 86 strikeouts below the league norm (actually, 86.45). His -86 ties the major league (post-1900) record; a couple of 19th century guys had bigger numbers. Anyway, Nate Cornejo (2003), Steve Kline (1972), Lew Burdette (1960) and Joe Niekro (1969) were all at -86, although Rueter actually has the biggest number if you carry out the decimals. I always knew there was something very unusual about Kirk Rueter as a pitcher.

Second, Cy Young in 1901 was 33-10, in 1902 32-11, 1903 28-9, 1904 26-16. In 1905 he was just 18-19, a losing pitcher, but had a career high in strikeouts, with 210. He was also 61 strikeouts above the league average that year, which was also a career high—61 strikeouts better than average, 58 walks better than average, but he had a losing record. That's tough.

That reminded me of something that I discovered in 1979, leafing through the old Macmillan Baseball Encyclopedia…no idea whether this is still true. I was wondering if there was any pitcher ever who led his league in both strikeouts per nine innings and fewest walks per nine innings.

The only pitcher who had ever done this, I concluded, was Walter Johnson—but he did it in his worst season. The only season between 1910 and 1925 that Johnson didn't have a winning record was 1920, when he was 8-10—but led the league in both strikeouts per nine innings (4.89) and fewest walks (1.69).

PART IV: SHAKESPEARE AND VERLANDER

American society could and should take lessons from the world of sports as to how to develop talent. How is it that we have become so phenomenally good, in our society, at developing athletes?

First, we give them the opportunity to compete at a young age.

Second, we recognize and identify ability at a young age.

Third, we celebrate their success constantly. We show up at their games and cheer. We give them trophies. When they get to be teenagers, if they're still good, we put their names in the newspaper once in a while.

Fourth, we pay them for potential, rather than simply paying them once they get to be among the best in the world.

The average city the size of Topeka produces a major league player every ten or fifteen years. If we did the same things for young writers, every city would produce a Shakespeare or a Dickens or at least a Graham Greene every ten or fifteen years. Instead, we tell the young writers that they should work on their craft for twenty or twenty-five years, get to be really, really good—among the best in the world—and then we'll give them a little bit of recognition.

The sporting world, meanwhile, gets criticized constantly for what we do so well. People get squeamish about young people being "too competitive", as if somehow this would damage their tender souls, and complain about the "undue attention" that is focused on young athletes. The grossest example is on the issue of race.

People in the sporting world in 1950 were just as racist as people in other parts of society—but people in the sporting world got over it a hell of a lot faster, because we cared more about winning than we did about discriminating. Because the sporting world was always ahead of the rest of the world in breaking racial barriers, black kids came to perceive sports as being the pathway out of poverty. For this we are now harshly and routinely criticized—as if it was our fault that the rest of society hasn't kept up. Some jackass PhD ex-athlete pops up on my TV two or three times a year claiming that a young black kid has a better chance of being hit by lightning than of becoming a millionaire athlete. This is nonsense as well as being a rational hash.

Look, it's not *our* fault that the rest of the world hasn't kept up. It's not *our* fault that there are still barriers to black kids becoming doctors and lawyers and airline pilots. Black kids regard the athletic world as a pathway out of poverty because it is. The sporting world should be praised and honored for that. Instead, we are more often criticized because the pathway is so narrow.

Which, I agree, is a real problem. I would never encourage my children to be athletes—first because my children are not athletes and second because there are so many people pushing to get to the top in sports that a hundred people are crushed for every one who breaks through. This is unfortunate. We are very good at producing athletes, and maybe we are too good at producing athletes. Sometimes the cost is too high. We should do more to develop the next Shakespeare and less to develop the next Justin Verlander.

But this situation is not a failing of the sporting world. Rather, it is that the rest of society has been too proud to follow our lead.

TSA

by Bill James

———

For the Harry Potter novels, J.K. Rowling invented a sport, Quidditch, which is played by magical peoples. But in inventing the sport she made an obvious mistake. She placed a very high value—150 points—on catching the golden snitch. What is obvious to a sports fan is that this would, in effect, make the game unplayable; the too-high value for the snitch would crush all of the other objectives of the sport, making the entire game revolve around capturing the snitch. In practice, *every* player would be basically committed to spotting the snitch, rather than just the Seeker, so that the game would not in fact play out the way Rowling assumes it would.

We are in the middle of a controversy about the Transportation Security Administration, having to do with unnecessary delays in flying and unnecessary invasions of privacy. I had something I wanted to say about this which seems so obvious to me that I am almost embarrassed to say it, but then none of them real smart talkin' heads says it, either, and I kind of think they've overlooked the obvious, so I'll go ahead.

Virtues are always in conflict with one another. Any two virtues that you can conceive of will at some point collide. If one seeks to be both honest and modest, you will find at some point—particularly if you're a really cool person like me—that you cannot be both honest and modest; you have to choose. If you attempt to be both fair and tolerant, if you attempt to be both generous and thrifty, if you attempt to be both open and cautious, if you attempt to be both clean and punctual or any combination of these, you will find that at some point these goals will collide and you must choose one or the other.

If, in the collision of virtues, you declare that the value of one virtue is infinite, then that virtue must always prevail. This means it will crush whatever other virtue it collides with. In real life this frequently has terrible consequences.

In the 1960s the Warren Court acted on the unstated assumption that a fair trial, free of certain flaws, was an infinite value—that whenever and wherever there was a taint upon a trial, the trial must be re-done. The ultimate consequence of this assumption was that tens of thousands of Americans became the victims of totally unnecessary violent crimes by ruthless criminals whose convictions and incarceration did not accord with the court's lofty standards. The courts acted as if a fair trial was an infinite value—and thus allowed the pursuit of better trials, free of certain abuses, to crush any competing values with which that one collided. Over the period of fifteen years it collided with the practical needs of law enforcement in a hundred different ways, and on every occasion the needs of law enforcement were crushed, since an infinite value always crushes whatever it collides with. Gradually, in a series of decisions beginning with *California v. Chapman* (1967) and culminating in *Arizona v. Fulminante* (1991), the high court placed limits on the infinite value of a fair trial, which allowed law enforcement to function rationally, which helped to bring the scourge of violent crime—unleashed by the Warren Court about 1963—under control.

At this point, speaking of fulminations, 30% of my audience will gasp in horror and attempt to instruct me on the "real" causes of the explosion in crime rates of the early 1960s...the baby boom, etc. To believe that demographic changes in the population caused the crime rate to explode is more ignorant than believing that Storm Davis was an outstanding pitcher when he went 19-7 in 1989. That's a political position, masquerading as a data analysis. It is—like the confidence of the Kansas City Royals in the value of a "winning" pitcher like Storm Davis—something that people choose to believe rather than facing the real facts and acknowledging the obvious conclusion.

Here (in the TSA controversy) we have a similar situation, with similarly disastrous consequences to which the Transportation Security Administration has chosen to blind itself. The TSA has placed an infinite value on the safety of each flight. In fact, the Federal Aviation Administration, since its founding in 1958, has placed an infinite value on the safety of each flight. What has been accomplished by this pursuit of perfection is stunning. The frequency of flight crashes has been reduced, and reduced, and reduced, and reduced, until an astonishing level of safety has been achieved. There hasn't been an airplane crash in the United States on a major carrier (knock wood) in more than nine years, since November, 2001. The policy of zero tolerance for risks of any kind, for the FAA, has been phenomenally successful, and, for whatever reason, has not clashed with any other values in a notable or harmful way.

The Transportation Security Administration also uses a zero-tolerance policy, but this unfortunately has collided with other values. The TSA places an infinite value on the safety of the airplanes, which means, unfortunately, that they place zero value on your time and your privacy—zero value, that is, relative to the value placed on the prevention of a terrorist event. Let us suppose that the value of each human life was put at $100 million, and let us suppose that 150 lives would be lost if there were a crash. The cost of an unfortunate event then could be placed at $15 billion; let's throw in another $5 billion for the cost of the airplane and the collateral damage on the ground, and make it $20 billion.

Well, what is the chance that Mrs. Esther Pugh, aged 93, flying from Ft. Lauderdale to Cleveland with her son Herbert, 61, is secretly a terrorist agent who will cause a plane crash if she is not thoroughly searched and humiliated before being allowed to the gate area? Let's say it is .000 000 000 001; in reality it is much less than that, but let's say. The cost of allowing her to proceed to the gate without any kind of security operation, then, could be estimated at $20,000,000,000 ($20 billion) times .000 000 000 001, or 2 cents. The cost of searching her—not the cost in terms of delays to others or the cost in terms of the value of privacy, but merely the cost in terms of hiring TSA workers to rummage through Esther's private possessions and feel up Esther's privates, plus the costs of their machinery and equipment—would probably be more like a dollar. Cost, $1.00. Benefit, 2 cents.

The only way this makes sense, then, is if we place an *infinite* value on the prevention of a terrorist act. If we place an infinite value on the prevention of a terrorist act, then the benefit is always greater than the cost, no matter *what* the cost might be.

Well, but what is the cost? The cost—as was the cost of the disastrous clumsiness of the Warren Court—is many human lives. American airline carriers carry about 800 million passengers a year. Let us estimate that the security apparatus wastes 10 minutes of each passenger's time per flight...the loss of 10 minutes of life for each flying customer, those 10 minutes being both unproductive and unpleasant. That is a gross loss of 8 billion minutes.

And how many minutes are a lifetime? Assuming that the average traveler would live another 40 years and not counting the time spent sleeping, we could say that each 14 million minutes would be a lifetime. The TSA is, in effect, killing about 570 people a year, ten minutes at a time. It's a conservative estimate; it doesn't include the time invested by the TSA employees themselves or, for example, the time that people lose by the need to be at the airport early to allow for the worst-case scenarios caused by airport security delays, or the time that is lost by taxpayers in earning the money that goes to pay the TSA to force us through time-consuming delays and humiliating searches.

The 570 lives is a conservative estimate, but the number is not the real point; the real point is that lifetimes are being lost while lives are being saved—and, therefore, that a rational accounting might be helpful. We have gotten into this pickle for a simple reason: we have placed an infinite value on one virtue—the safety of flights. All virtues collide at some point, and, when an infinite value collides with any other value, it is as if the other value did not exist, since it does not matter what the other value might be.

(This article grew out of a conversation with my son, Isaac. Isaac objects that in fact the FAA's zero tolerance policy for risk has had very high costs in its collision with other virtues. We should now be able to fly from San Francisco to Paris, he argues, in an hour or so, by having airplanes that rocketed into space. We are unable to do so because the FAA's insistence on zero risk has inhibited innovation, forcing us to fly around on 20-year-old airplanes because those are the only airplanes that the FAA is certain are 100% safe. Objection noted.)

———··———

HOT PITCHERS

by Bill James

If a starting pitcher has been pitching well in his recent starts, is he more likely to pitch well today? It is hard to believe that he isn't, isn't it? If a pitcher has pitched shutout baseball in three of his last four starts, don't you *have* to believe that he's more likely to pitch well than if he's been getting beat up?

A pitcher being "hot" is a little different than a hitter being hot. A hitter being hot...what is that? Self-confidence? Karma? Extra batting practice? A new titanium necklace? A pitcher can be hot or cold for meaningful and apparent reasons—minor injuries, arm fatigue, a new pitch that's working for him that the league hasn't figured out yet.

I have done three new studies to try to figure out whether a "hot" starting pitcher is more likely to pitch well, in his next start, than a pitcher who has not been pitching well. In the first of those studies, what we will call the Bob Gibson Study, I studied the performance of "hot" pitchers versus the performance of equally good pitchers who were not hot. In the second study, which we will call the A. J. Burnett/Josh Beckett study, I studied the question of whether there was any tendency for good games and bad games to form clusters. My third study compared pitchers with identical or near-identical year-to-date records, but one of whom came into the start hotter than the other. I call this the Matched-Set Study.

I. THE BOB GIBSON STUDY

I took all pitchers from the years 1960 to 1969, and divided them into two groups, twice. The first division was among pitchers as to the quality of the season's performance. I ranked all pitchers by the Season's Score, and then divided them into eight groups with (essentially) equal numbers of games started in each group. There were 31,730 Games Started in major league baseball from 1960 to 1969, so that's about 4,000 starts in each group.

Then I divided the 4,000 starts in each set into eight groups, separated by how "hot" the pitcher was coming into the game.

The highest quality pitchers, coming into the game red hot, would be group AA. The highest quality pitchers, coming into the game having been pitching very badly, would be group AH.

The lowest quality pitchers, coming into the game having been pitching very badly, would be group HH. The lowest quality pitchers, coming into the game pitching very well, would be group HA.

There were 64 groups of starting pitchers, with about 500 starts in each group.

This is coloratura, but you may be wondering who is an "A" quality starting pitcher, who is a "B", etc. The Season Score is based on the pitcher's Wins, Losses, Innings Pitched, ERA, Strikeouts and Walks, and also on Saves if there are any. Here is a chart of randomly selected "A", "B", "C", pitchers, etc., which should give you a sense of what kind of pitcher we are dealing with in each group.

	First	Last	Year	G	IP	W	L	WPct	SO	BB	ERA
	Denny	McLain	1968	41	336	31	6	.838	280	63	1.96
	Jim	**Kaat**	**1966**	**41**	**305**	**25**	**13**	**.658**	**205**	**55**	**2.75**
A	Tom	Seaver	1968	36	278	16	12	.571	205	48	2.20
	Vern	**Law**	**1960**	**35**	**272**	**20**	**9**	**.690**	**120**	**40**	**3.08**
	Steve	Barber	1963	39	259	20	13	.606	180	92	2.75
	Don	Drysdale	1960	41	269	15	14	.517	246	72	2.84
	Don	**Mossi**	**1961**	**35**	**240**	**15**	**7**	**.682**	**137**	**47**	**2.96**
B	Mickey	Lolich	1965	43	244	15	9	.625	226	72	3.43
	Larry	**Jackson**	**1963**	**37**	**275**	**14**	**18**	**.438**	**153**	**54**	**2.55**
	Lew	Burdette	1961	40	272	18	11	.621	92	33	4.00
	Dave	McNally	1965	35	199	11	6	.647	116	73	2.85
	Fred	**Newman**	**1964**	**32**	**190**	**13**	**10**	**.565**	**83**	**39**	**2.75**
C	Ray	Sadecki	1968	38	254	12	18	.400	206	70	2.91
	Hank	**Aguirre**	**1965**	**32**	**208**	**14**	**10**	**.583**	**141**	**60**	**3.59**
	Bill	Stafford	1962	35	213	14	9	.609	109	77	3.68

	First	Last	Year	G	IP	W	L	WPct	SO	BB	ERA
	Jim	Merritt	1968	38	238	12	16	.429	181	52	3.25
	Jim	**Coates**	**1961**	**43**	**141**	**11**	**5**	**.688**	**80**	**53**	**3.45**
D	Joe	Niekro	1967	36	170	10	7	.588	77	32	3.34
	Al	**Downing**	**1965**	**35**	**212**	**12**	**14**	**.462**	**179**	**105**	**3.40**
	Dick	Ellsworth	1964	37	257	14	18	.438	148	71	3.75
	Chris	Short	1962	47	142	11	9	.550	91	56	3.42
	Ken	**Johnson**	**1964**	**35**	**218**	**11**	**16**	**.407**	**117**	**44**	**3.63**
E	Frank	Baumann	1962	40	120	7	6	.538	55	36	3.38
	Ray	**Sadecki**	**1963**	**36**	**193**	**10**	**10**	**.500**	**136**	**78**	**4.10**
	Wade	Blasingame	1964	28	117	9	5	.643	70	51	4.23
	Cal	Koonce	1965	38	173	7	9	.438	88	52	3.69
	Ray	**Washburn**	**1965**	**28**	**119**	**9**	**11**	**.450**	**67**	**28**	**3.63**
F	Tom	Murphy	1969	36	216	10	16	.385	100	69	4.21
	Ernie	**Broglio**	**1964**	**29**	**170**	**7**	**12**	**.368**	**82**	**56**	**3.82**
	Eli	Grba	1962	40	176	8	9	.471	90	75	4.55
	Barry	Latman	1966	31	103	2	7	.222	74	35	2.71
	Bill	**Monbouquette**	**1966**	**30**	**103**	**7**	**8**	**.467**	**61**	**22**	**4.72**
G	Jim	Shellenback	1969	38	102	4	7	.364	57	52	3.88
	Lew	**Krausse, Jr.**	**1967**	**48**	**160**	**7**	**17**	**.292**	**96**	**67**	**4.28**
	Jack	Fisher	1962	32	152	7	9	.438	81	56	5.09
	Arnold	Earley	1963	53	116	3	7	.300	97	43	4.73
	Marcelino	**Lopez**	**1967**	**8**	**27**	**1**	**2**	**.333**	**21**	**19**	**4.72**
H	Larry	Miller	1965	28	57	1	4	.200	36	25	5.05
	Jack	**Kralick**	**1965**	**30**	**86**	**5**	**11**	**.313**	**34**	**21**	**4.92**
	Mike	Marshall	1969	20	88	3	10	.231	47	35	5.13

To determine how "Hot" a pitcher was coming into the game, I used a method which is conceptually simple, but which will entangle us in an undesirable number of details. It was based on Game Scores. Game Scores are a method that "score" each start by a starting pitcher essentially on a zero-to-one-hundred scale. To convert this into a "Hot Pitcher Scale", each pitcher's score after each game (and thus, heading into his next start) was 20% of his score from his last start, plus 80% of whatever his score was prior to his last start.

For illustration, Bob Gibson, heading into his start of June 6, 1968, had a "Heat Index" of 69.4, which means that he had been pitching very, very well indeed up to that time. On June 6 he pitched a 3-hit shutout, Game Score of 84, which increased his Heat Index to 72.3—.80 times 69.4, plus .20 times 84. On June 11 he pitched a 5-hit shutout, striking out 4, for a Game Score of 79, increasing his Heat Index to 73.6. On June 15 he pitched a 4-hit shutout, striking out 13 batters and walking no one, for a Game Score of 92. This increased his Heat Index to 77.3. On June 20 he pitched a 5-hit shutout, striking out 6, Game Score of 82. This increased his Heat Index to 78.3. On June 26 he pitched a 4-hit shutout, striking out 7, Game Score of 86. This increased his Heat Index to 79.3.

On July 1, 1968, he pitched a complete game, but gave up 9 hits and a run, for a Game Score of "just" 67. This knocked his Heat Index down to 77.2, but he followed that up on July 6 with a 6-hit shutout, striking out 9, Game Score of 80, which pushed him back up to 77.8. His Game Scores in his next four starts were 85, 86, 82 and 80 (four complete games in there, with a total of two runs allowed), which pushed his Heat Index up to 80.7.

On August 4 he pitched his worst games in months. He pitched 11 innings and struck out ten batters, but he did give up 5 runs, 4 of them earned, Game Score of 62. This cut his Heat Index down to 77.0. Then, however, he began to rebuild it, pitching two more shutouts in his next three starts, Game Scores of 84, 71 and 92, which put him at 79.9.

On August 24 he struck out 15 batters but gave up 6 runs, Game Score 70, which cut him back down to 77.9. On August 28, however, he pitched a 4-hit shutout, striking out 14 batters, Game Score 90. This pushed him up to 80.3 On September 2 he pitched a ten-inning, 4-hit shutout, Game Score 89. This put him at 82.1.

This frankly incredible run of games—12 shutouts in 19 starts—made Gibson at that moment, heading into his next start, the hottest pitcher of the 1960s, and probably one of the hottest pitchers in the history of baseball. But the 1960s were a pitching-dominated era in which pitchers completed games, and there were *many* hot streaks by pitchers in the 1960s which were comparable to this—none equal, but many close. The hottest starting pitchers of the 1960s, not making redundant mentions of Gibson or other pitchers on the same streak, were:

1. Bob Gibson, September 6, 1968   82.1
2. Juan Marichal, May 31, 1966   81.1
3. Luis Tiant, July 7, 1968   80.9
4. Larry Dierker, September 17, 1969 79.3
5. Gaylord Perry, September 15, 1967 79.3
6. Sandy Koufax, July 12, 1962   78.5
7. Sandy Koufax, August 18, 1965   77.4
8. Ray Culp, September 29, 1968   77.3
9. Don Drysdale, June 8, 1968   76.8
10. Sandy Koufax, June 14, 1966   73.5

The dates given are their highest scores entering a game, thus their highest scores AFTER the previous game. The coldest pitchers of the 1960s were:

1. Lew Burdette, July 30, 1965   28.7
2. Galen Cisco, September 21, 1962   30.6
3. Craig Anderson, August 7, 1962   31.7

The ugly and annoying details of this system have to do with the start of a player's career, or the start of a season. I started each pitcher out at 50.00 each season if

a) he made his first start of the season before May 1, and
b) had made a start in the previous season.

If he had no major league starts the previous season, or if he made his first start of the season on May 1 or later, then he started the season at 40.00. Trust me, there is research that justifies the distinction, and it doesn't really matter after about eight starts; the "starting point" disappears pretty quickly, taking a 20% hit in each start.

Also, to avoid getting non-representative scores for early-season, 1960, I included 1959 data into the study for the purpose of establishing the "Heat Indexes", although I did not include the games played in 1959 in the study for purposes of output data.

Anyway, at the conclusion of this I had 64 groups of pitchers, coded AA, AB, AC, AD, AE, AF, AG, AH, BA, BB...HE, HF, HG, HH. AA was high-quality pitchers who came into the game hot; HH was low-quality pitchers who came into the game pitching badly, even by their own standards. We had about 500 starts in each group of games. The essential question was whether and to what extent pitchers would pitch better, relative to the quality of their overall performance, when they were "hot" than when they were "cold".

They did not pitch better. The extent to which they pitched better was "zero", or, actually, negative.

The top-end pitchers (the "A" quality pitchers) actually did pitch better when they were "hot" than when they were "cold". This group of pitchers made 486 starts when they were "hot" (Group AA), of which they won 260, lost 150 (.634 percentage), struck out 3,133 batters, walked only 893, and posted a 2.35 ERA. When they were "cold" (Group AH), they made 506 starts, struck out only 2,557, walked 998 and posted a 2.63 ERA, although they did post an even better won-lost record when "cold" (AH) than when "hot" (AA). They were 285-112 (.718) when they came into the outing cold.

This chart gives their average Game Score, by group:

Code 1	Code 2	GS	G Score Average
A	A	485	64.46
A	B	499	62.09
A	C	446	60.01
A	D	500	61.70
A	E	500	62.81
A	F	510	61.70
A	G	522	60.09
A	H	506	60.58

As you can see, their Game Scores were higher when they were "hot".

This, however, was the exception within the study. In all other groups, the pitchers pitched better when they came into the start "cold" than when they came in "hot".

There is a "natural" or "grouping" effect that would explain this phenomenon. By grouping pitchers based on their end-of-season stats, we put them on a fixed-point course. If they had pitched well in the past, they *had* to pitch less well in the future in order to reach their fixed point by the end of the season, and vice versa.

I knew that this would occur, but it was my judgment that this effect was would be small enough that the tendency of hot pitchers to continue to pitch well—the tendency of starts to cluster—could fairly easily shine through it if that effect was of any significance. Maybe I was right about that; maybe I was wrong. In any case it didn't. Consistently, the pitchers in each group pitched better when they came into the game "cold" than when they came into the game "hot".

(The aberration in Group A could be explained by the fact that this was an open-ended group, a group with a fixed bottom but an open top, so that the difference between the top and bottom pitchers in the group was larger than in any of the other groups.)

II. THE JOSH BECKETT / A.J. BURNETT STUDY

Josh Beckett and A. J. Burnett were teammates and starred together on the Florida Marlins years ago, and for the last several years have pitched for rival teams in the American League East. They have similar career records and had somewhat similar seasons in 2009, Beckett going 17-6 with a 3.86 ERA, Burnett going 13-9 with a 4.04 ERA.

Their seasons, however, were very different in this respect: that Beckett was obviously streaky during the 2009 season, while Burnett was up and down. This chart gives the Game Scores for Beckett and Burnett start by start, with "Hot" or "Cold" for the next game under each (with a blank for a Game Score of 50, which is by definition neither hot nor cold):

A. J. BURNETT
Game Scores over 33 Starts

51	76	50	19	49	54	44	55	41	69
Hot			Cold		Hot	Cold	Hot	Cold	Hot

56	28	73	62	82	62	49	44	60	74
Hot	Cold		Hot			Cold		Hot	

18	77	45	61	17	65	22	65	41	62
Cold	Hot	Cold	Hot	Cold	Hot	Cold	Hot	Cold	Hot

55	66	49
Hot	Cold	

JOSH BECKETT
Game Scores over 32 Starts

76	43	47	14	21	44	50	61	74	71
Hot	Cold						Hot		

76	76	29	84	71	48	57	88	58	58
Hot		Cold	Hot		Cold	Hot			

68	74	68	25	37	41	49	55	58	63
Hot			Cold				Hot		

46	39
Cold	

If you subtract the value of each Josh Beckett start from the value (Game Score) of the previous start, you get a total of 473. If you do the same for Burnett, you get a total of 786.

We can extend that measurement another step. If you subtract the Game Score for every Josh Beckett start from the Game Score for every other Josh Beckett start, you have 496 possible comparisons, which average 21.44. But if you subtract only the *consecutive* starts, you get a lower figure, 15.26. The second figure is lower because each start tends to be like the start before it.

If you do the same for Burnett, you get an average of 19.66 for all matches, but 24.56 for the consecutive-game matches. The consecutive-game average is higher because Burnett tended to follow a good start with a bad start.

Beckett's games formed clusters. Burnett's did not. If starting pitchers in fact have any tendency to get "hot" and "cold"—as Beckett did—then their "consecutive game" average will be lower than their "random match" average (understanding that we are not actually dealing with randomly matched games, but with the average for all games that could be randomly matched.)

If there is no tendency for pitchers to be hot or cold, then the averages will be the same.

I figured these averages for all starting pitchers for the years 2000 to 2009. Let's deal only with the pitchers who made 25 or more starts, since that's complicated enough. The streakiest starting pitcher of those ten years was Dan Haren in 2007, with the A's. Haren finished the season 15-9 with a 3.07 ERA. Through his first

14 starts, Haren posted a 1.58 ERA. For his last 20 starts, his ERA was 4.22. A hot period; a cold period. These were the ten "streakiest" pitchers of the last decade, in single seasons:

	Year	First	Last	Starts	Consecutive Game Average	Random Match Average	Ratio
1	2007	Dan	Haren	34	8.2	14.0	.582
2	2004	Johan	Santana	34	11.9	19.2	.620
3	2004	Paul	Wilson	29	14.4	21.0	.686
4	2003	Mark	Mulder	26	15.2	22.1	.690
5	2003	Matt	Morris	27	15.0	21.0	.711
6	2009	Josh	Beckett	32	15.3	21.4	.712
7	2003	Livan	Hernandez	33	12.5	17.2	.727
8	2002	Paul	Wilson	30	13.7	18.7	.730
9	2007	Sergio	Mitre	27	13.7	18.7	.732
10	2009	Kevin	Millwood	31	12.2	16.3	.749

While these were the ten "most inconsistent" or "least streaky" pitchers:

	Year	First	Last	Starts	Game Average	Random Match Average	Ratio
1	2002	Vicente	Padilla	32	24.6	19.0	1.29
2	2004	Matt	Morris	32	27.0	21.2	1.27
3	2005	Kevin	Millwood	30	17.9	14.2	1.26
4	2004	Curt	Schilling	32	23.7	18.9	1.25
5	2009	A.J.	Burnett	33	24.6	19.7	1.25
6	2005	Tomo	Ohka	29	22.4	18.0	1.25
7	2005	Jamey	Wright	27	27.3	23.0	1.24
8	2006	Aaron	Cook	32	21.0	16.9	1.24
9	2002	Danys	Baez	26	18.8	15.2	1.23
10	2006	Clay	Hensley	29	21.2	17.2	1.23

If the pitchers' Game Scores have any tendency to form clusters, this method will result in a ratio less than 1.000. If there is no such tendency, this method will result in a figure higher than 1.000 as often as a figure lower than 1.000, and the overall figure will be 1.000.

OK, we come then to the question: Is there, in general, any tendency for Game Scores to form clusters?

None whatsoever.

Well, OK, we can't say that it is zero. There may be some very small tendency for games to form clusters. In the decade as a whole the average for comparisons of consecutive starts, based on a total of 45,588 observations, was 18.79. The average for randomly matched starts by the same pitcher, based on a total of 581,121 observations, was 18.92. The overall ratio isn't 1.000; it's 0.993.

Among pitchers with 25 starts or more, the observed effect was even smaller than that. There were 983 pitchers in the years 2000 to 2009 who made 25 or more starts. 488 of them had "clustering ratios" less than 1.00, indicating some streakiness. 495 had clustering ratios higher than 1.00. For these pitchers, the overall ratio was not 1-.993, but 1-.9992. Whether this difference is statistically significant would not seem to matter since, even if it is statistically significant—which I doubt—the difference is so small that it could still easily be explained by some "loading" factor such as ERAs being higher in mid-summer.

III. THE MATCHED-SET STUDY

As I said earlier, my third study compared pitchers with identical or near-identical year-to-date records, but one of whom came into the start hotter than the other. For example, John Maine after his start of September 5, 2007, was 14-9. Roy Oswalt, after his start of September 6, 2008, was also 14-9. Maine had made 28 starts; Oswalt had made 28 starts. Maine had an ERA of 3.80; Oswalt, 3.72. Maine had 146 strikeouts; Oswalt had 144. There records were, for all practical purposes, the same.

However, Oswalt was at that moment red hot. In his last eleven starts, he was 8-1, and had cut his ERA during that stretch from 4.77 to 3.72. In his last start (the September 6 start) he had pitched a 1-hit shutout. In the start prior to that, he had pitched 8 and a third innings of shutout baseball. In the start before that, he had given up one run in 7 innings. Two starts before that, he had pitched 8 innings of one-hit, shutout baseball, striking out ten. He was sizzling.

Maine was not. In his September 5 start he had given up 9 hits and 6 runs in four and a third innings. Two starts prior he had given up 6 runs in five and a third innings. Over his last eleven starts he was 4-5, and his ERA had gone *up* from 2.71 to 3.80. He was struggling. His overall record was the same as Oswalt's, but his recent performance was very different.

From the years 2000 to 2009, I identified 504 "matched sets" like this in which two starting pitchers had nearly-identical records, but one was hot and the other was not. Details:

In order to be considered a set, the pitchers had to have exactly the same won-lost records—same wins, same losses.

The difference between them in ERA had to be no greater than 20 points (actually, no greater than 0.205).

The difference between them in games started could be no greater than two.

The difference between them in strikeouts could be no greater than 10%. (Actually, 10% of the higher figure. If one pitcher had 180 strikeouts and the other had 163, that would qualify because the difference is less than 10% of the higher figure.)

Also, the starts had to occur at the same time of the season, with a difference of no greater than 10 as the "team game number" for the season. (In other words, I didn't want to compare a pitcher from September with a pitcher with an identical record in July, since this might introduce other issues into the comparison.)

I didn't use any comparisons in which pitchers had made fewer than ten starts.

I figured how "hot" each pitcher was in the same way as the earlier study, except that I started everybody off at 50.00, rather than starting some guys off at 40.00 as in the previous study. (Since every pitcher was at least ten starts into the season, the initial starting point is no longer of much relevance. If I had started pitchers off at 75.00, I'd have gotten basically the same results.) To qualify for the study, one of the matched-set pitchers had to have a "Hot Score" at least seven points higher than the other one, going into his next start.

Also, a pitcher couldn't be matched against himself in the same year...in other words, Roy Oswalt as of September 6, 2008, couldn't be matched against Roy Oswalt as of September 1, 2008. Pitchers could, however, be matched against themselves in a different season, if they had near-identical records in different seasons, but were "hot" in one season and "not hot" in another. This did happen numerous times—that pitchers wound up matched against themselves in other seasons. For example:

- Randy Johnson as of September 5, 2000, had made 30 starts with a won-lost record of 17-6, 2.45 ERA, 299 strikeouts.
- Randy Johnson as of September 7, 2001, had also made 30 starts with the same won-lost record (17-6), same ERA (2.45), but 320 strikeouts. But he was ten degrees hotter at that time in 2001 than he was in 2000.

....

- Greg Maddux as of September 7, 2001, was 17-8, 30 starts, 2.93 ERA, 162 strikeouts.
- Greg Maddux as of September 13, 2000, was 17-8, 32 starts, 3.00 ERA, 168 strikeouts. But he was eight degrees hotter in 2001 than he was in 2000.

....

- Russ Ortiz, as of August 14, 2001, had made 25 starts and was 13-6, 3.46 ERA, 116 strikeouts.
- Russ Ortiz as of August 15, 2004, had made 25 starts and was 13-6, 3.31 ERA, 124 strikeouts. But Ortiz was nine degrees hotter in 2004 than he was in 2001.

I should explain also that these records are the pitchers' records as *starting* pitchers. A handful of these pitchers may also have made a relief appearance or two, creating some small differences in ERA or occasionally even a win or a loss. Anyway, here are 38 more randomly selected matches:

Month	Day	Year	First	Last	GS	IP	W	L	WPct	SO	BB	ERA	
9	19	2001	Matt	Morris	31	197.7	20	7	.741	161	47	3.10	Hot
9	12	2008	Brandon	Webb	31	205.7	20	7	.741	168	59	3.28	Not

Month	Day	Year	First	Last	GS	IP	W	L	WPct	SO	BB	ERA	
9	23	2000	Greg	Maddux	34	244.3	19	8	.704	183	40	2.91	Hot
9	24	2002	Roy	Oswalt	33	229.0	19	8	.704	202	61	2.95	Not

Month	Day	Year	First	Last	GS	IP	W	L	WPct	SO	BB	ERA	
9	17	2005	Cliff	Lee	30	187.3	17	4	.810	136	49	3.75	Hot
9	10	2004	Mark	Mulder	29	210.0	17	4	.810	131	76	3.90	Not

Month	Day	Year	First	Last	GS	IP	W	L	WPct	SO	BB	ERA	
9	17	2004	Roy	Oswalt	32	216.3	17	9	.654	189	57	3.49	Hot
9	30	2001	Tim	Hudson	34	229.0	17	9	.654	175	70	3.42	Not

Month	Day	Year	First	Last	GS	IP	W	L	WPct	SO	BB	ERA	
9	25	2001	Wade	Miller	30	200.0	16	8	.667	168	70	3.56	Hot
9	15	2002	Matt	Morris	30	197.3	16	8	.667	163	62	3.42	Not

Month	Day	Year	First	Last	GS	IP	W	L	WPct	SO	BB	ERA	
9	27	2005	Tim	Wakefield	32	220.3	16	11	.593	150	68	3.96	Hot
9	24	2000	Livan	Hernandez	32	232.0	16	11	.593	162	71	3.84	Not

Month	Day	Year	First	Last	GS	IP	W	L	WPct	SO	BB	ERA	
9	17	2001	Robert	Person	30	190.3	15	6	.714	168	74	4.02	Hot
9	14	2009	Jered	Weaver	30	194.0	15	6	.714	164	61	3.85	Not

Month	Day	Year	First	Last	GS	IP	W	L	WPct	SO	BB	ERA	
9	21	2008	Bronson	Arroyo	33	193.0	15	11	.577	158	66	4.66	Hot
9	28	2001	Ryan	Dempster	33	210.7	15	11	.577	170	106	4.66	Not

Month	Day	Year	First	Last	GS	IP	W	L	WPct	SO	BB	ERA	
8	28	2004	Pedro	Martinez	27	180.7	14	5	.737	188	46	3.69	Hot
9	2	2009	Josh	Beckett	27	181.3	14	5	.737	172	48	3.87	Not

Month	Day	Year	First	Last	GS	IP	W	L	WPct	SO	BB	ERA	
9	15	2006	Bronson	Arroyo	32	221.3	14	9	.609	172	55	3.17	Hot
9	18	2008	Cole	Hamels	32	220.3	14	9	.609	189	52	3.10	Not

Month	Day	Year	First	Last	GS	IP	W	L	WPct	SO	BB	ERA	
7	26	2006	Justin	Verlander	20	130.3	13	4	.765	88	36	2.69	Hot
7	18	2002	Bartolo	Colon	20	146.3	13	4	.765	91	43	2.64	Not

Month	Day	Year	First	Last	GS	IP	W	L	WPct	SO	BB	ERA	
8	22	2001	Javier	Vazquez	28	193.7	13	11	.542	183	41	3.76	Hot
8	28	2007	Daisuke	Matsuzaka	27	176.3	13	11	.542	174	66	3.88	Not

Month	Day	Year	First	Last	GS	IP	W	L	WPct	SO	BB	ERA	
8	3	2009	Matt	Cain	22	148.0	12	3	.800	117	54	2.25	Hot
7	26	2007	Dan	Haren	22	149.0	12	3	.800	118	39	2.42	Not

Month	Day	Year	First	Last	GS	IP	W	L	WPct	SO	BB	ERA	
8	27	2004	Derek	Lowe	26	151.7	12	10	.545	85	58	5.22	Hot
8	21	2001	Mike	Hampton	26	164.3	12	10	.545	91	66	5.26	Not

Month	Day	Year	First	Last	GS	IP	W	L	WPct	SO	BB	ERA	
7	19	2001	Freddy	Garcia	20	135.3	11	2	.846	79	45	3.46	Hot
7	9	2006	Tom	Glavine	19	119.0	11	2	.846	82	36	3.48	Not

Month	Day	Year	First	Last	GS	IP	W	L	WPct	SO	BB	ERA	
7	15	2006	Curt	Schilling	20	134.3	11	3	.786	124	16	3.42	Hot
7	15	2006	Mike	Mussina	20	128.3	11	3	.786	113	24	3.30	Not

Month	Day	Year	First	Last	GS	IP	W	L	WPct	SO	BB	ERA	
9	8	2006	Livan	Hernandez	30	189.0	11	12	.478	115	65	5.10	Hot
9	3	2003	Jason	Jennings	30	170.3	11	12	.478	113	84	5.13	Not

Month	Day	Year	First	Last	GS	IP	W	L	WPct	SO	BB	ERA	
6	29	2009	Roy	Halladay	15	109.0	10	2	.833	95	14	2.56	Hot
6	24	2004	Roger	Clemens	15	95.7	10	2	.833	101	38	2.73	Not

Month	Day	Year	First	Last	GS	IP	W	L	WPct	SO	BB	ERA	
8	30	2000	Darren	Dreifort	26	154.7	10	7	.588	132	69	4.36	Hot
9	1	2000	Randy	Wolf	27	174.3	10	7	.588	136	70	4.34	Not

Month	Day	Year	First	Last	GS	IP	W	L	WPct	SO	BB	ERA	
9	11	2004	Sidney	Ponson	29	189.7	10	14	.417	103	60	5.31	Hot
9	15	2006	Ramon	Ortiz	30	178.3	10	14	.417	97	62	5.30	Not

Month	Day	Year	First	Last	GS	IP	W	L	WPct	SO	BB	ERA	
7	19	2002	Kyle	Lohse	20	110.7	9	5	.643	71	43	4.80	Hot
7	23	2004	Esteban	Loaiza	20	133.7	9	5	.643	78	43	4.85	Not

Month	Day	Year	First	Last	GS	IP	W	L	WPct	SO	BB	ERA	
9	3	2008	Barry	Zito	28	153.7	9	16	.360	98	89	5.45	Hot
9	3	2004	Darrell	May	27	160.3	9	16	.360	97	49	5.61	Not

Month	Day	Year	First	Last	GS	IP	W	L	WPct	SO	BB	ERA	
5	26	2001	Curt	Schilling	11	84.3	8	1	.889	93	11	2.77	Hot
5	26	2002	Randy	Johnson	11	79.0	8	1	.889	100	22	2.73	Not

Month	Day	Year	First	Last	GS	IP	W	L	WPct	SO	BB	ERA	
8	6	2004	Mike	Maroth	23	149.7	8	7	.533	70	43	4.45	Hot
8	5	2007	Jason	Marquis	23	133.3	8	7	.533	73	55	4.39	Not

Month	Day	Year	First	Last	GS	IP	W	L	WPct	SO	BB	ERA	
9	19	2001	Albie	Lopez	30	183.7	8	18	.308	118	70	5.10	Hot
9	27	2001	Bobby J.	Jones	32	192.3	8	18	.308	113	35	5.05	Not

Month	Day	Year	First	Last	GS	IP	W	L	WPct	SO	BB	ERA	
6	22	2001	CC	Sabathia	14	76.0	7	2	.778	55	37	4.38	Hot
6	10	2008	Chien-Ming	Wang	14	90.0	7	2	.778	51	35	4.30	Not

Month	Day	Year	First	Last	GS	IP	W	L	WPct	SO	BB	ERA	
6	15	2007	Derek	Lowe	15	102.3	7	6	.538	72	31	3.08	Hot
6	19	2002	Al	Leiter	15	93.7	7	6	.538	74	28	3.07	Not

Month	Day	Year	First	Last	GS	IP	W	L	WPct	SO	BB	ERA	
8	19	2000	Steve	Parris	25	145.0	7	14	.333	86	50	4.78	Hot
8	23	2005	Brett	Tomko	24	145.7	7	14	.333	84	48	4.94	Not

Month	Day	Year	First	Last	GS	IP	W	L	WPct	SO	BB	ERA	
5	30	2007	Chris	Young	11	67.0	6	3	.667	60	26	2.42	Hot
5	29	2001	Kevin	Brown	10	65.7	6	3	.667	64	17	2.60	Not

Month	Day	Year	First	Last	GS	IP	W	L	WPct	SO	BB	ERA	
7	31	2001	Glendon	Rusch	22	119.3	6	6	.500	101	29	4.60	Hot
7	30	2005	Jose	Contreras	21	125.7	6	6	.500	92	56	4.58	Not

Month	Day	Year	First	Last	GS	IP	W	L	WPct	SO	BB	ERA	
8	8	2008	Joe	Blanton	24	149.0	6	12	.333	76	43	4.71	Hot
8	10	2005	Brian	Lawrence	24	150.0	6	12	.333	79	38	4.80	Not

Month	Day	Year	First	Last	GS	IP	W	L	WPct	SO	BB	ERA	
7	29	2003	Darrell	May	20	127.7	5	5	.500	65	34	3.81	Hot
8	4	2007	Sergio	Mitre	20	117.7	5	5	.500	67	26	3.67	Not

Month	Day	Year	First	Last	GS	IP	W	L	WPct	SO	BB	ERA	
6	3	2000	Kenny	Rogers	11	78.7	5	5	.500	32	17	4.00	Hot
5	30	2003	Jeff	Suppan	11	67.0	5	5	.500	35	18	4.03	Not

Month	Day	Year	First	Last	GS	IP	W	L	WPct	SO	BB	ERA	
8	22	2006	Jeff	Weaver	24	131.0	5	13	.278	83	35	6.11	Hot
8	22	2000	Masato	Yoshii	25	147.3	5	13	.278	78	44	5.99	Not

Month	Day	Year	First	Last	GS	IP	W	L	WPct	SO	BB	ERA	
6	5	2001	Jarrod	Washburn	10	64.7	4	4	.500	39	26	4.45	Hot
5	27	2005	Tim	Wakefield	10	62.3	4	4	.500	39	30	4.48	Not

Month	Day	Year	First	Last	GS	IP	W	L	WPct	SO	BB	ERA	
7	8	2005	Nate	Robertson	17	102.0	3	7	.300	59	38	3.35	Hot
7	3	2002	Chris	Reitsma	17	94.0	3	7	.300	55	32	3.45	Not

Month	Day	Year	First	Last	GS	IP	W	L	WPct	SO	BB	ERA	
9	14	2008	Jeremy	Sowers	20	109.0	3	8	.273	60	34	5.70	Hot
9	6	2000	John	Snyder	20	110.7	3	8	.273	61	69	5.86	Not

Month	Day	Year	First	Last	GS	IP	W	L	WPct	SO	BB	ERA	
6	12	2000	Frank	Castillo	12	65.0	2	5	.286	50	34	4.71	Hot
6	9	2002	Shawn	Estes	12	69.0	2	5	.286	52	35	4.83	Not

Obviously, Jeremy Sowers in mid-September, 2008, wasn't too hot, or he wouldn't have been 3-8 with a 5.70 ERA, but he was hotter than Snyder. Sowers' ERA on July 19, 2008 was 6.44. Snyder's ERA had been 4.76 on July 8, but it had gone up to 5.86. You get my point. One was hotter than the other.

You may be wondering whether the 504 qualifying matches that I found are all there are. The answer to that is "no"; you could find 2,000 matches from the years 2000 to 2009 as good as these, if you worked at it hard enough. In this study, each group of 504 pitchers had an aggregate won-lost record of 4637-3779, and each group had an aggregate ERA of 4.12.

Anyway, I then looked at how these pitchers performed in their next start, and also compared their final season stats.

In this study the pitchers who were "hot" *did* out-perform the pitchers who were not hot in their next starts, and over the balance of the season—not by a huge amount, but they did outperform them. The "hot" pitchers, in their 504 "next starts", had a won-lost record of 199-175, an ERA of 4.28, and an average Game Score of 50.62.

The "cold" pitchers, in their 504 next starts, had a won-lost record of 177-177, an ERA of 4.74, and an average Game Score of 47.94.

At season's end the "hot" pitchers had an average season score of 119.1. The pitchers who were "cold" had an average season score of 112.8.

———·———

Of course, I should point out...I never know whether to point out things that any intelligent person could see for himself. I always feel like I'm insulting your intelligence when I point out things like this, but when I don't point them out, somebody always explains it to me as if I was the idiot who didn't get it.

I should point out that this difference, even assuming it to be statistically significant, is not necessarily evidence of a "hot streak/cold streak" phenomenon. Players' levels of ability do change over time. The ten best pitchers in baseball today are not the same ten guys that you would have listed five years ago. It may be that, when you measure equal performers but split according to recent performances, *some* of the pitchers who have pitched well recently have actually improved, while others have actually declined.

In any case, suppose that you are going to a ballgame tomorrow, and both starting pitchers are 11-7 with ERAs of 3.45, but one of them is hot and the other is cold. Is the one who is "hot" more likely to win the game?

Yes.

———·———

Justice McReynolds and Buck O'Neil

by Bill James

My great-grandmother's maiden name was McReynolds. When my father was a little boy there was a picture of the Supreme Court in the newspaper one day, and his grandmother showed him the picture, and pointed to Justice James Clark McReynolds. There, she said—that's my cousin; that's your cousin. Supreme Court Justice McReynolds.

They were poor, rural people living hundreds of miles from the seats of power, not the kind of people that you would ordinarily think would have a relative on the Supreme Court, and so we were always rather quietly proud of this.

What we did not know, unfortunately, was that Justice McReynolds was a horrible bigot. I read several books a year about the Supreme Court. In the last three months I have read *The Rehnquist Choice: The Untold Story of the Nixon Appointment that Redefined the Supreme Court*, by John Dean, and *Minnesota Rag: The Dramatic Story of the Landmark Supreme Court Case That Gave New Meaning to Freedom of the Press*, by Fred Friendly. As McReynolds was basically the only unrepentant racist to serve on the Supreme Court in the modern era, books about the Supreme Court very often will invent some way to tell some ripping tales about McReynolds' boorishness and intolerance, even if their book really has nothing to do with McReynolds. He was colorful and different, and people like to talk about him, much in the way that the pig that wandered into church during the sermon and dropped a load right in front of the altar was colorful and different, and one might imagine that the people who were in church on that Sunday morning would probably talk about it for the rest of their lives.

Over time, these stories seem to be gathering steam. Justice McReynolds vigorously objected to Jews being on the Supreme

Court or anywhere else that he had to deal with them, and he made no secret of his objections. When Justice Brandeis was selected to the Supreme Court, McReynolds refused to attend his swearing-in ceremony, refused to shake his hand, refused to travel with him, and refused for several years even to speak to him. Supreme Court conferences—then and now—begin with each justice shaking hands with each other judge, but McReynolds refused to shake Brandeis' hand. There is a traditional Supreme Court photograph taken at the beginning of each term, but in 1924 McReynolds refused to be photographed with Brandeis. He refused to sign opinions that Brandeis had authored, even if he agreed with them.

I read that, when Brandeis spoke in conference, McReynolds would get up and leave the room, but I never heard this until recently and am not convinced that it is true. When Benjamin Cardoza was elected to the Supreme Court some years later, McReynolds did attend the swearing-in ceremony, but pointedly read a newspaper as Cardoza took the oath.

My good cousin objected to women as attorneys, and he accepted blacks only in servile positions. He thought wearing fingernail polish was vulgar, and he would ridicule men who wore wrist watches, which he thought were effeminate. Because of this behavior, McReynolds is often singled out for censure, and people will quite often say that he was the worst Supreme Court Justice of all time. This is not exactly true—in fact, I would argue that he was, all things considered, a better Supreme Court Justice than any of the string of losers appointed to the court by Harry Truman. Despite his personal failings he was in many ways a competent judge, and at times, particularly early in his career, a progressive judge. He was also, perhaps, not quite as much of a pig as the church goers remember that he was. Oliver Wendell Holmes was quite fond of him, and William O. Douglas remembered him warmly and wrote of him that, when leading the court due to the absence of the Chief, "he was the soul of courtesy, graciously greeting and raptly listening to the arguments by lawyers of both sexes."

Anyway, reading McReynolds' entry in Wikipedia, I was struck by this passage:

> In addition, he hated tobacco and forbade smoking in his presence. He is said to have been responsible for the "No Smoking" signs in the Supreme Court building, which was inaugurated during his tenure. He would announce to any Justice who attempted to smoke in Conference that "tobacco smoke is personally objectionable to me." Few

Justices would try, and those who did "were stopped at the threshold."

Well...but isn't that the attitude that *everybody* has about smokers anymore? Don't almost all people nowadays object to smoking in their presence? Isn't Wikipedia just piling on here, faulting McReynolds for being ahead of his time as an anti-smoking activist? If McReynolds wasn't a universal object of contempt, might he not be singled out for praise in this regard, rather than condemnation?

And if Justice McReynolds is excused on this count because he was merely on the wrong side of a line drawn across history, then shouldn't it be pointed out as well that, with regard to the other attitudes that we now condemn, Justice McReynolds as well was merely on the wrong side of a line drawn across history? After all, the attitudes that he had toward Jews and blacks and working women, in the time and place where he grew up, were the universal attitudes that everybody held...that is, everybody who counted. Everybody who was white, male and Protestant. McReynolds' only fault was that he held on to these attitudes after others had discarded them.

Well...no.

Of course Justice McReynolds' bigotry cannot be so easily excused. Intolerance of people is different than intolerance of bad habits. McReynolds was a Supreme Court Justice, a thinking man and a leader. He is held to a higher standard than the conventions of time and place. He is expected to search for truth and to see the truth when it shines so brightly in front of him. He is expected to promote justice. He is not expected to be a defender of injustice.

But I always think of Buck O'Neil, and of Buck's conviction that there is enough good in any white man that you can reach out to him. Buck would have embraced James McReynolds, and there is a 50/50 chance he would have made him his friend.

Buck was a tremendously effective warrior against racism, and part of that was that he battled against the racism, rather than the racist. To recognize that there is good in everyone is also to recognize that there is evil in everyone—that the sins of Justice McReynolds and Bull Connor live deep within each of us, asking quietly to be fed. To talk *too much* about the racism of others, I think, is a kind of self-righteousness, an effort to deny our own sins by talking loudly about others'.

———·—

Olympic NASCAR Racing

by Bill James

Special Rules

1. Style points will be given both for laying rubber and for accelerating quickly without laying rubber.

2. All pit crews must wear ice skates and carry plastic clothes hangers.

3. Each style point will be equivalent to one MPH of speed sustained over a short-term burst of 7/10 of a second or longer and across a distance greater than 200 feet, unless somebody can figure out what this means, in which case we reserve the right to change or re-interpret this rule in mid-contest.

4. Try not to run over Dick Button; he's had a hard life.

5. Style points will be given by the judges for:
   - Stopping suddenly without fishtailing.
   - Lighting a pipe while driving over 125 miles per hour.
   - Rolling down your passenger's side window with your right hand while fighting off an effort to pass you on the left.
   - Adjusting your rear-view mirror with a Swiss Army knife.
   - Technical excellence.

6. Latvian auto racers are allowed to race with a Pomeranian hanging his head out the window to feel the wind, as is traditional in Latvia.

7. Modest donation to Olympic cause required for each commercial sponsor.

8. Garage will be referred to as "Grand Olympic Automotive Aegean Repair Facility".

9. All drivers must stop on the 47th lap and run across the track in front of the other cars.

10. Don't ask why.

11. 47-point penalty for looking like you might ask why.

12. Engine blocks must be entirely constructed of recycled laptop computers.

13. All racers required to use the terms "Grandeur" and "Festival" in all pre-race and post-race interviews.

14. All cars required to display prominently the name of 19th-century Tibetan monk, Chequenunga Tuk, who invented NAS-CAR but had the idea stolen from him by evil Americans.

15. Style points will be deducted for:
    - Taking your hands off the wheel.
    - Spitting out the window.
    - Forgetting your Swiss Army knife.
    - Running over Dick Button.
    - Discourteous driving.

16. Every third lap must depart track to use jumping ramps. Points awarded for air time: 7 foot = 4.2 miles per hour at 8 seconds.

17. Drivers must scrub and wax jumping ramp after every jump.

18. All drivers required to make annual trek to pay homage to grave of Juan Antonio Samaranch.

19. If awarded medal, must be able to detach the steering wheel and carry it with you to the medal stand.

20. No driving too fast; somebody might get hurt.

The Greatest Pitchers' Duels of the 1980s

by Bill James

In any ten-year period, there are a large number of absolutely fantastic pitcher's duels in the major leagues. You want an example? OK, on August 26, 1987, Cleveland met Milwaukee in Milwaukee, Teddy Higuera against John Farrell. Farrell pitched nine innings of three-hit shutout baseball, striking out seven and walking only two. He was the lesser of the two. Higuera pitched ten innings of three-hit shutout baseball, striking out ten. Doug Jones relieved Farrell in the tenth inning, gave up a run with one out in the bottom of the tenth, and lost the game, 1-0.

That wasn't the punch line; that was the setup. This is the punch line: on a listing of the greatest pitchers duels of the 1980s, that ranks #50. There are 49 pitchers duels, in the 1980s, better than that one.

OK, how do we decide what is the best pitcher's duel of the 1980s? Who is to say that one pitcher's duel is better than another?

Obviously, the decision involves near-arbitrary choices—but there *is* a rational basis to separate one from another. A two-hit shutout is better than a three-hit shutout. Ten shutout innings are better than nine. A three-hitter with 10 strikeouts is better than a three-hitter with 9 strikeouts. A pitcher's duel between Roy Halladay and CC Sabathia is better, other things being equal, than a pitcher's duel between Ross Detwiler and Garrett Mock. These are not difficult things to agree upon.

The arbitrary part comes when we have to choose between a three-hitter with 10 strikeouts and a two-hitter with 7. Which is better? If you have a game between Roy Halladay and Ross Detwiler and a game between CC Sabathia and Garrett Mock, which is better? It's arbitrary.

It's arbitrary, of course, *but we can nonetheless choose*. You're free to argue, you're free to disagree, you're free to make up your own list. This is my list, and I have a rational basis for it.

Let us say that there are four elements that make a classic pitcher's duel:

1) Quality starting pitchers,
2) Outstanding performances by those starting pitchers,
3) Quality performances by other pitchers appearing in the game, other than the two starters, and
4) A low score.

With the help of Retrosheet and my son Isaac, who created a spreadsheet for me that has the information I need, I ranked every major league game played during the 1980s as a pitcher's duel, giving each one a "pitcher's duel score". Here's how I did it:

1. QUALITY OF STARTING PITCHERS.

For this, I used the pitcher's Season Score. I wanted the first three factors above to be essentially even as influences on the outcome of the process, so I converted the Season Score to a zero-to-hundred scale by the following method. The best pitcher's season of the 1980s was by Dwight Gooden in 1985, when he went 24-4 with a 1.53 ERA. That's a Season Score of 449. The worst pitcher's season of the 1980s was by Mike Parrott in 1980, when he went 1-16 with an ERA of 7.28. That's a Season Score of -113. We'll set Gooden equal to 100 and Parrott equal to zero, and scale everybody else between them. The "score" for each pitcher is his Season Score, plus 113, divided by 562, times 100, converted into an integer.

For the game above, Teddy Higuera was 18-10 in 1987—a good pitcher—but with a not-too-great 3.85 ERA. That's a Season Score of 210, which becomes 58 on our converted scale. John Farrell, on the other hand, was a recent callup (making his second major league start). He finished the season 5-1 with a 3.39 ERA, but still, as a late-season callup his Season Score was 67, which becomes 32 on the conversion scale. It's 58 against 32, which is still good; that's a total of 90. The average for a game in the 1980s was 76.

The *worst* pitching matchup of the 1980s occurred on July 1, 1986, when John Butcher of the Indians squared off with Rick Langford of the A's at Cleveland's cavernous park. John Butcher in 1986 was 1-8 with a 6.56 ERA—and he was the better starting pitcher in the game. Langford was 1-10 with a 7.36 ERA. That is a *bad* pitching matchup, although Butcher pitched a shutout and the Indians won the game 9-0. That was Butcher's win for the year, and the last win of his major league career.

On the other end of that scale, in Busch Stadium on September 11, 1985: Dwight Gooden faced off against John Tudor. Gooden, as we mentioned, was having the best season of any major league starter in that decade—but Tudor wasn't chopped condiments, either. He was 21-8 with a 1.93 ERA. This ranks, actually, as the sixth-best season by a starting pitcher in the 1980s. In other words, although Tudor couldn't win the Cy Young Award because he was going head to head with Gooden, he was actually *better* than 75% of the Cy Young pitchers of the 1980s.

At this point you may ask "Why stop with the Season Score? Why not look at the pitcher's entire career? Wouldn't John Tudor be more impressive, after all, if he was Jim Palmer or Tom Seaver?"

He would indeed, and there is no reason you couldn't score the pitchers on that scale if you chose to. I just did not have the data to do that in my spreadsheet, and I don't *know* whether it would be better or not, so I didn't include it. But there's no reason you couldn't.

2. THE QUALITY OF PERFORMANCE OF THE STARTING PITCHERS.

The quality of the performance we evaluated by Game Scores, which are sort of on a zero-to-100 scale to begin with, so we didn't have to convert them.

I remember this game, and many of you will remember it as well. The worst performance of the 1980s by two starting pitchers in the same game occurred on June 26, 1987 at Fenway Park. The pitchers that day were two guys who might well meet up someday in Cooperstown: Tommy John and Roger Clemens. Both were having pretty good years. Tommy John, 44 years old at that time, nonetheless finished the season 13-6 with a 4.03 ERA, and Clemens...well, Clemens was *always* having a good season, and would win the Cy Young Award that year.

On that day, however, neither pitcher had his mojo working. Boston scored four runs in the first, and five more in the second—two of them off of John, and the other three off of the bullpen. Clemens, staked to a 9-0 lead after an inning and a half, gave up eight runs in the bottom of the third, the Yankees claiming an 11-9 lead by the end of the inning. The Yankees eventually won it in extra innings, 12 to 11. Game Scores: John, 8, Clemens, 8.

On the other end of that scale: Floyd Youmans against Nolan Ryan in the Astrodome, July 22, 1986. Through nine innings the game was nothing-nothing. Youmans had given up two hits, no walks, eight strikeouts. It was the only complete game of his career in which Youmans didn't walk anybody—but he didn't win. Nolan Ryan was Ryanesque. Through 9 innings Ryan had given up only

1 hit, only 2 walks, and had struck out 14 batters. Both pitchers—working on a one-hitter and a two-hitter—stayed in the game into the tenth. Ryan got one more out in the tenth but walked two and was replaced by Dave Smith, who got out of the inning un-scored on. Glenn Davis homered for the Astros leading off the bottom of the tenth, and the Astros' won, 1-0. Through the first nine innings the two pitchers combined had allowed 3 hits and 2 walks, and had struck out 22. Game Scores: Youmans, 85, Ryan, 96.

3. Quality Performances by Other Pitchers in the Game.

In Montreal on August 23rd, 1989, Orel Hershiser pitched 7 shutout innings for the Dodgers, giving up 4 hits and striking out 6—a fine performance, I am sure you would agree, but not quite on the level of Nolan Ryan in one of his crazy near-no-hitters. Pascual Perez, pitching for Montreal, matched Hershiser inning for inning, giving up 7 hits but no runs through 8 innings.

Hershiser, however, gave way to Jay Howell, who pitched two shutout innings, getting the Dodgers through nine. Perez gave way to Tim Burke, who matched Howell with two shutout innings of his own. Howell was replaced by Alejandro Pena, who shut down the Expos for four more innings. It took two Smiths to equal one Pena—two shutout innings for Montreal by Bryn Smith, two more by Zane. It was nothing-nothing through 13 innings. Pena was replaced by Tim Crews, who blanked Montreal for three more innings—but the Smiths were replaced by Rich Thompson, who pitched six innings of shutout relief, the finest performance of his major league career.

John Wetteland came in for Los Angeles; he was a rookie then, and had been a starter for the previous month. He pitched a shutout inning, and another, and another, and another. Through 18 innings it was scoreless, 19, 20. In the 21st inning a starter came in for Montreal, Dennis Martinez. Wetteland wound up pitching 6 shutout innings, giving the bullpen 15 on that day.

Finally, in the top of the 22nd inning, Rick Dempsey hit a home run. The Dodgers won it, 1-0 in 22 innings. Montreal pitchers struck out 17 batters in the game, walked none—and lost.

Doesn't that HAVE to be the greatest pitcher's duel of the decade? 22 shutout innings, 21 by the other team—how can you beat that?

I can see an argument for that position, but this is the way I see it. The concept of a "duel" implies a one-on-one matchup. When the bullpens are impressive—certainly when they are *this* impressive—that counts *toward* the game being an all-time great pitcher's duel, but it isn't *exactly* what we mean by the term. What we mean by the term is one on one, *mano a mano*, Dennis Weaver against the mad truck driver.

I gave credit for the performance of other pitchers in the game, in this way. First, I figured the "Game Score" for all pitchers in the game, *as if they were one pitcher*. (I say "I" figured it...actually, Isaac figured it, but whatever.) The Dodgers pitched 22 innings in that game, striking out 18, walking 6, giving up 13 hits and no runs. If one pitcher did that, that would be a Game Score of 138, so I entered that as "138", even though this violates the essence of the Game Score concept, which is intended to assess the performance of a single pitcher.

Team Game Scores, figured in this way, no longer stay within the bounds of zero and one hundred—not that they *always* do, anyway, but they do more than 99.9% of the time. Team Game Scores for the 1980s ranged from 138 to minus 76—a spread of 214 points. I thus converted them into a "team performance score", for our present purposes, by adding 76 points and dividing by two. The Dodgers for this game get 107 points; the worst performance of the decade gets zero. The worst performance of the decade was the Mets against the Phillies, June 11, 1985, a game lost 26-7.

I said that I wanted the three elements to be equal, but that's not exactly true; I want the performance of the pitchers to count more than their identity. In games where only two pitchers work, this element becomes a redundant counting of the second element, and often gives about the same score by the two methods.

4. Pulling it Together.

The "Pitcher's Duel Score" for any game is the sum of these three scores outlined above, minus five points for each run that is scored in the game. (If there is a great pitcher's duel but somebody scores 7 runs off a reliever in the 9th inning, it rather mars the performance.)

There were 20,337 regular-season major league games in the 1980s. I scored each of those. You remember the Teddy Higuera/John Farrell matchup I talked about earlier? That scores at 428:

> 58 points for Teddy Higuera's performance on the season,
>
> 32 points for John Farrell's performance on the season,
>
> 94 points for Teddy Higuera's performance in the game (his Game Score was 94),
>
> 86 points for John Farrell's performance in the game,
>
> 85 points for the performance of all Milwaukee pitchers in the game,

78 points for the performance of all Cleveland pitchers in the game,

Minus 5 points for the one run that was eventually scored in the game.

These are the top ten pitcher's duels of the 1980s:

10. May 9, 1988, Boston at Kansas City (Clemens against Gubicza)

Here's something you may not remember: Roger Clemens was supposed to pitch against Mark Gubicza in Kansas City on April 27, 1986, but the game was rained out. Clemens then made his start against Seattle two days later, striking out 20 hitters and emerging as a star.

Clemens had only 19 major league wins before that, but I was already a huge Roger Clemens fan, having met him when he just out of college and then having seen him dominate the Royals in August, 1984. I had tickets to the game that was rained out in KC, and then I was in Boston on a book tour on April 30, 1986, so I just missed the historic 20-strikeout game on both ends.

Anyway, the Clemens/Gubicza duel finally came off on May 9, 1988. Gubicza was actually better that year than Clemens was; Clemens was 18-12 with a 2.93 ERA and threw 8 shutouts (!), but Gubicza was 20-8 with a 2.70 ERA and threw 4 shutouts of his own. But Clemens was better on this day. The game was scoreless through five innings. Marty Barrett reached on an error leading off the sixth, and scored an un-earned run on a two-out triple by Mike Greenwell. The Red Sox scored again in the 9th, Gubicza putting the runner on, the bullpen letting him in. Clemens, on the other hand, allowed nothing: three hits, one walk, sixteen strikeouts.

My wife and I didn't see this game, I'm sure. Isaac was born two days later. The game scores at 447 on our pitcher's duel score—141 points for the quality of the two pitchers who started the game, plus 159 points for the performance of the two starting pitchers (Clemens' Game Score was 96), plus 157 points for the performance of all pitchers in the game, minus 10 points for the two runs that were scored.

9. September 16, 1988, Los Angeles at Cincinnati
(Tom Browning against Tim Belcher)

There was a two-and-a-half-hour rain delay at the start of the game, and then there was a dual no-hitter through five innings. Browning never did give up a hit; he pitched a perfect game—27 men up, 27 down—making his record at that point 16-5. He finished 18-5. Belcher gave up an un-earned in the sixth, three hits finally, one walk. He also faced only 27 batters in an eight-inning complete-game loss.

The game scores at 452 by our system—120 points for the quality of the two pitchers, plus 174 points for the performance of the two starting pitchers (Browning's Game Score was 94), plus 163 points for the performance of all pitchers in the game, minus five points for the one run that was scored.

8. August 23, 1989, Los Angeles at Montreal
(Orel Hershiser against Pascual Perez)

This is the game I talked about earlier that was scoreless through 21 innings, finally won by the Dodgers on a home run in the 22nd inning.

The game scores at 453 points in our system—103 points for Hershiser against Perez, 148 points for the performance of the two starting pitchers, plus 207 points for the performance of all pitchers in the game, minus five points for the run that was scored.

7. September 5, 1980, Philadelphia at Los Angeles
(Don Sutton vs. Steve Carlton)

Sutton had the lowest ERA in the majors that year, 2.20; Carlton had the second-lowest, 2.34, was 24-9 and won the National League Cy Young Award. Ron Cey hit a second-inning home run for the only run of the game. Sutton pitched 8 shutout innings, giving up 3 hits and striking out 10.

The game scores at 454 points in our system—154 points for the fact that it is Sutton vs. Carlton, 150 points for the performance of the two starting pitchers, 155 points for the performance of all pitchers in the game, minus five points for the one run that was scored.

6. September 21, 1981, Philadelphia at Montreal
(Steve Carlton vs. Ray Burris)

Carlton didn't win the Cy Young Award in 1981 although he was still probably the best pitcher in the league. Fernando Valenzuela was an early-season sensation, and rode the wave of popularity this generated to the Cy Young Award, not that he wasn't pretty good, also. Carlton was 13-4 in the strike-shortened season, 2.42, ERA; Ray Burris was nowhere near as good in general but was awfully good on this particular day.

Both Burris and Carlton pitched 10 innings of 3-hit, shutout baseball, Carlton striking out a dozen hitters. They turned the game over to the bullpens in the eleventh, and the bullpens kept it scoreless through 16. Andre Dawson drove in a run with a single with one out in the bottom of the 17th, winning the game 1-0. Bryn Smith, who also pitched in the long game against the Dodgers eight years later, was the winning pitcher—his first major league win.

The game scores at 455 points—100 points for the quality of the two starting pitchers, plus 178 points for the performance of the two starting pitchers, plus 182 points for the performance of all pitchers in the game, minus five points for the one run that was scored.

5. Bastille Day, 1985, the Mets at Houston
(Dwight Gooden vs. Bob Knepper)

The game was nothing-nothing through seven. Billy Doran threw the ball away after a force play at second base, allowing an un-earned run to score, the only run of the game. Gooden pitched a 5-hit shutout and struck out 11.

The game scores at 465 points—148 points for the quality of the two starting pitchers, plus 162 points for the performance of the two starting pitchers, plus 160 points for the performance of all pitchers in the game, minus five points for the run.

4. October 1, 1985, Mets at St. Louis
(Ron Darling against John Tudor)

We probably should give some extra points for the fact that the pennant was on the line, but we don't. Darling was the Mets' #2 starter that year, finishing 16-6 with a 2.90 ERA; Tudor, as we mentioned earlier, was the #2 pitcher in the league.

October 1 was a Monday, and there was a week left on the schedule. The Cardinals came into the game with the best record in the National League, 98-58; the Mets were three games behind them at 95-61. Darling pitched nine shutout innings. Tudor pitched ten. Jesse Orosco pitched a scoreless tenth inning, and a scoreless eleventh. Darryl Strawberry homered off of a reliever with two out in the top of the eleventh, and the Mets won it, 1-0.

The game has a "pitcher's duel score" of 470—148 points for the quality of the two starting pitchers, plus 165 points for the performance of the two starting pitchers, plus 162 points for the performance of all pitchers in the game, minus five points for the run.

3. September 28, 1988, Los Angeles at San Diego (Andy Hawkins against Orel Hershiser)

Orel Hershiser entered the game with a string of 49 consecutive shutout innings. The major league record was 58, set by Don Drysdale twenty years earlier. Hawkins was decent, too; he was 14-11 that year, 3.35 ERA.

The Dodgers had clinched the division, and would go on to win the World Series. On this day, however, Hershiser and Hawkins each pitched ten innings of 4-hit shutout baseball. Hershiser's ten shutout innings gave him 59 in a row, a major league record which still stands, as he did not pitch again during the regular season. The ubiquitous Jesse Orosco came in for the Dodgers, followed by Tim Crews and Ken Howell. Mark Davis and Lance McCullers matched them for San Diego, and the game was nothing-nothing through 15 innings.

Finally, in the top of the 16th inning, the Dodgers manufactured a run against Dave Leiper on a single, two groundouts and an error by late-season callup Bip Roberts, who had entered the game as a pinch-runner in the 11th inning. Roberts then singled, leading off the bottom of the 16th and giving him a chance to redeem himself, but was caught stealing, leaving the Padres with two outs, nobody on base. Carmelo Martinez walked, and Ricky Horton replaced Ken Howell on the mound for the Dodgers. Mark Parent, pinch-hitting for San Diego, drilled a two-run home run, and San Diego won the game, 2-1.

We give this one a pitcher's duel score of 478—133 points for Hershiser against Hawkins, plus 174 points for the ten shutout innings by each starting pitcher, plus 186 points for the performance of all pitchers in the game, minus 15 points for the three runs that were eventually scored.

2. September 6, 1985, New York at Los Angeles
(Fernando Valenzuela against Dwight Gooden)

Fernando in 1985 had arguably his best major league season, finishing 17-10 with a career-best 2.45 ERA, 208 strikeouts in 272 innings. Both teams were in the pennant race, the Dodgers a few games in front in their division, the Mets coming in a game and a half behind the Cardinals.

Gooden pitched 9 shutout innings, striking out 10 batters. That's not bad, but Fernando was better; he pitched 11 shutout innings. Gooden turned it over to Roger McDowell, Terry Leach and the ubiquitous Jesse Orosco, who pitched shutout ball through 13 innings. Darryl Strawberry hit a 2-run single with two out in the top of the 13th, and the Mets won it, 2-0.

We have this one scored at 496—169 points for the quality of the starting pitchers, plus 174 points for the quality of their performance, plus 163 points for the performance of all pitchers in the game, minus ten points for the two runs that were scored.

1. September 11, 1985, St. Louis at New York
(Dwight Gooden against John Tudor)

This was Gooden's next start, five days after the duel with Valenzuela.

You may be wondering why I started this study with the 1980s. I started it with the 1980s because, in the 1980s, it was clear to me before I started what the right answer for the best pitcher's duel of the decade should be. This game is hard to beat.

With Gooden starting against Tudor, that was not only the best starting pitching matchup of the decade, but the best regular season starting pitching matchup that was possible during the decade. We give the game 185 points (out of a possible 200) for the quality of the two starting pitchers.

Did the pitchers pitch well? Oh, pretty well. Gooden pitched nine shutout innings once again, giving up five hits as he had against the Dodgers. He would pitch a 2-hit shutout in his next start, giving him a 31-inning scoreless streak at that point. The streak was ended by an un-earned run, and, following the un-earned run, Gooden would pitch another 17 consecutive scoreless innings.

Tudor answered with a 10-inning, 3-hit shutout of his own, striking out 7—which was also his third consecutive shutout; his streak also would end at 31 innings. Tudor's Game Score that day was 91; Gooden's was 81. That's a total of 172.

That wasn't the best performance by two starting pitchers in the decade; that would be Nolan Ryan against Floyd Youmans, as we talked about earlier. It wasn't the best performance, but it was the 16th best. In the 20,337 regular-season games during the decade, the Tudor/Gooden game ranks #1 in terms of the quality of the two starting pitchers, and #16 in terms of the quality of their performance.

Gooden finished 24-4 in 1985, yet here are two consecutive games in which he pitched 9 innings, did not give up a run, and did not get a win. It's an unusual thing; when a pitcher pitched 9 innings and did not give up a run, in the 1980s, he won the game a little more than 96% of the time. The odds of doing it twice in a row and not winning either game are 700-to-1—assuming you can pitch two consecutive shutouts. You can look at Gooden, if you choose, not as a 24-4 pitcher, but as a 26-4 pitcher who had some unusual tough luck.

Gooden turned over his game to—who else?—Jesse Orosco, and Orosco gave up a leadoff home run to Cesar Cedeno. The game scores at 513 by our system—185, plus 172, plus 161 for the performance of all the pitchers in the game, minus five points for the run that was scored.

I used to work with somebody who had a poster on his office wall based on an aerial photo taken in the 9th or 10th inning of this game; it's driving me batty, but I can't remember who it was. I can remember spending many hours looking at that poster, but I can't place it. It may have been Josh Byrnes, or it may have been Rob Neyer. The game was in the middle of a pennant race, and it is a famous game at a certain level. By our system it is easily the greatest pitcher's duel of the 1980s, and one of the greatest of all time.

CODA

As this article appeared in Bill James Online, I had intended to do the best pitcher's duels of each decade from 1950 to the present, although I think at some point everybody got bored with the project and we failed to finish it. Those of you who live in the present are probably wondering what the best pitchers duels of 2010 were, to which the answers are:

    a) The best pitching matchup of 2010, in terms of having two great pitchers on the mound, was June 15 at Yankee Stadium, Roy Halladay against CC Sabathia. The Yankees shelled Halladay; Sabathia was pretty good.

    b) The best pitching performance of 2010, in terms of having two starting pitchers who pitched great, was July 10th at Philadelphia, Roy Halladay against Travis Wood of Cincinnati. Both Halladay and Wood pitched 9 innings of shutout ball, Halladay giving up five hits, Wood only one.

c) The five best pitchers duels of 2010, considering all facets and starting at the top, were:

1. September 13 at Tampa Bay, CC Sabathia against David Price. Price and Sabathia pitched eight innings of shutout ball each, Sabathia giving up 2 hits and Price 3. Tampa Bay won the game, 1-0 in eleven innings, on a pinch hit home run by Reid Brignac.

2. May 29 at Miami, Roy Halladay against Josh Johnson. Halladay pitched a perfect game; Johnson lost it on an un-earned run.

3 The Travis Wood/Roy Halladay game, mentioned above.

4. The Mets at St. Louis, April 17, Johan Santana against Jaime Garcia. Santana and Garcia both yielded after seven shutout innings, but each team then got eleven shutout innings out of the bullpen. The Mets finally won it, 2-1 in 20 innings.

5. Roy Halladay against Josh Johnson again, June 10 in Philadelphia. Johnson won the re-match, 2-0.

———•———

TIPPING

by Bill James

———

How old are you? If you are less than 30, I would argue that in your lifetime, the United States government will outlaw giving or receiving tips.

At the time of World War II the standard tip for service was 5%. Just after the war it shifted upward to 10%, and, in the mid-1960s, to 15%. I remember Ann Landers advising her readers that "inflation hits everybody; the waitress's costs have gone up, too." There is an obvious logical short-circuit here; if inflation hits everybody, the waitress's 10% automatically goes up. But anyway, tipping went to 15% by 1970, and, in the last few years, has moved to 20%.

At the same time, the number of things that one is expected to tip *for* grows constantly. I delivered pizzas for Pizza Hut in the mid-1970s; we never got tips and never expected them. I remember a couple of people offered to tip me, but I turned them down because it didn't seem right. In the 1980s the people who drove car rental company courtesy vans were forbidden from accepting tips; now they have tip jars. Tip jars are turning up everywhere; even bakeries have tip jars. Mm, that was a good doughnut. Drop your change here.

Hotel room service has developed layers of redundant service fees—a room service fee, plus a gratuity, PLUS a line for you to write in your own tip. Wait a minute…how does the "gratuity" differ from the tip? I thought the gratuity *was* the tip. A $7 breakfast costs $20, plus $15 in tips. Forty years ago the only people you tipped were waiters and cab drivers and bell boys; now you tip your roofer and movers and lawn mowers and barbers and bar tenders.

A few old tipping jobs have disappeared…elevator operators and gas pump servicemen, for example. We pump our own gas, now, and push our own elevator buttons. I should stress that I am not angry about this, or annoyed about it, or anything of the sort; this is not an angry or complaining article. It is a rational observation article. Tipping is growing taller and wider and heavier, and growing in comparison to almost anything else, for an obvious reason: it cuts out the IRS. It's economically efficient because, as a practical matter, tips aren't reported or are heroically under-reported to the IRS. If the car rental company pays the van driver $40,000 a year, the IRS is there with its hand out, wanting their cut; if the car rental company pays him $30,000 a year and he makes $10,000 in tips, he winds up with more money because he tells the IRS that he made only $117.22 in tips.

How much do I tip, in the course of a year? I don't know, but it has to be thousands of dollars. Tipping is treated as a test of generosity, thus as a test of values. Major league baseball players tip clubhouse attendants hundreds of dollars a week. If you don't tip well, you're a nasty, wasty skunk who doesn't care about the little guy. My observation about this is not that it is right or that it is wrong, but that it is growing, that it has been growing for a long time, and that it will continue to grow until it forces the country to take action to stop it. It isn't a question of *if* the standard tip will go to 25%, but *when*. It isn't a question of *whether* more and more people will begin to expect tips, but merely of *who* they will be. The people who book appointments at dentist offices? Dry cleaners? Airline stewards and stewardesses? Bag boys? Oh, wait a minute; in some grocery stores, they already do.

The growth of tipping, which is normally done in cash because the IRS can't track all the cash, is at odds with the movement of the country toward a cash-less society. I would argue that at some point the growth of the tipping industry *has* to stop; logically, I don't see how it can just continue to grow, unchecked, for another 50 or 60 years. The question, really, is whether the government will step in and put a stop to it, or something else will.

It may be that the restaurants will get organized and put a stop to tipping, or the hotels, or the rental car companies. It may be that one of them will get organized and take the lead, and the others will follow. Arthur Bryant's Bar-B-Q in Kansas City, has a sign: "If anyone in this establishment asks you for or accepts a tip, please let us know and that person will be fired immediately." It may be that the movement toward a cash-less society will eventually enable the IRS to track all tips or almost all tips, thus removing the economic advantage of tipping as opposed to paying wages, thus draining the swamp.

But I doubt it. I think eventually society will have to step in, declare tipping to be an onerous and unlawful activity, and put a stop to it. I predict that this will happen before 2050.

———

THE MINOR LEAGUE PYRAMID

by Bill James

———

I don't know why it took me until I was 61 years old to realize this, but...does it occur to anyone but me that it is very unnatural to have a minor league system which is *not* in the shape of a pyramid?

This occurred to me recently, when the discussions arose about a pyramid-shaped Hall of Fame, while I was also doing some work on the minor leagues. The minor leagues, as they arose in nature, were rather in the shape of a pyramid, in that there were a lot of bad leagues for each good league. The leagues in their early history did not have classifications or grades...that arose about 1905; when the leagues were organized into levels there were more teams at the lower levels than at the higher levels.

When Branch Rickey began taking control of minor league teams to create an organized farm system (mid-1920s), his system was a pyramid. As late as the mid-1950s, the Dodger farm system retained a distinct pyramid shape. The switch from a pyramid-shaped to a tube-shaped farm system (by which I mean that there are as many teams at higher levels as at lower levels) occurred from about 1945 to about 1965, as four things happened:

1. Large numbers of minor league teams died,

2. Expansion, urbanization and television ate up many of the minor league markets,

3. The major leagues gained full control over the surviving minor league teams, and

4. The major league teams, acting in concert, began to coordinate minor league policies.

When major league farm directors thought about a farm system, they thought it should be sort of like a school system, where a student proceeds from Grade 6 to Grade 7 to Grade 8; a player would proceed from Low A to High A to Double-A to Triple-A. They also thought that this would save them money; in fact, they still think that. If you talk to a farm director about adding a second team in Low A, what he will probably say is, "We don't have enough real prospects to fill up one team in Low A. What do we need with a second one?"

I would argue that a tube-shaped minor league system is artificial, and that this constricts the flow of talent to the major leagues, and causes numerous other real-life problems. Let us say that a major league player is at level 100, a Triple-A player at level 90, a Double-A player at 80, etc. A tube-shaped minor league system is artificial because, in fact, there are many, many more players at level 60 than at level 80, and many more players at level 80 than at level 100; and it is dysfunctional because, in fact, players do not progress normally from level 60 to level 70, level 70 to level 80. *Some* players progress from 60 to 70 and from 70 to 80, of course, but as many players do not progress from each level as do, so that if you have a hundred players at level 60, you'll get 5 to 8 at level 100.

This simple fact—which I suspect few people would deny—makes it unnatural to have a tube-shaped minor league system, and this creates a system in which teams are always trying to force players up from the bottom, rather than allowing them to rise naturally. This allows "cavities" to form at the higher levels, which of course has happened. Since teams generally have only two to five minor league prospects who are near the level of major-league ready—two to five prospects at "90"—Triple-A baseball has been taken over by non-prospects hanging around, waiting for somebody at the major league level to drop dead. This has caused the relative quality of Triple-A baseball vs. the majors to slide backward, which has made the step up from the minors to the majors a larger step, which creates problems for major league teams. Even Double-A teams are largely populated by what could be called lower-class Triple-A players—players not quite good enough to hang around and hope at the Triple-A level.

A second problem with the current system is that it cuts off the development of a certain type of player—what could be called the Enos Slaughter/Pete Rose type of player. In my youth there were players around, like Tony Gonzalez, Johnny Temple, Wally Moon, Dick McAuliffe, Bob Skinner, Smoky Burgess, Don Mincher and Cesar Tovar, who really didn't seem to possess outstanding ability, and who would never have been high draft picks or received large bonuses in the current system. Pete Rose and Enos Slaughter were like that, although they had very successful careers. What made these players stand out was not that they ran terribly fast or threw tremendously well or were big and strong, but that, when you put them in uniform and let them play, they succeeded. They compensated in determination, adaptability and competitiveness for what they lacked in more obvious ability.

There are still some of those type of players around, like Jed Lowrie and Brandon Inge, but not so many of them; our system now is not good at identifying or developing that type of talent. This leads to a third problem with the current system: that it designates "stars" too early in their progress, contributing to an entitlement mentality among athletes who have been designated for stardom from an early age. There is a fourth problem, which I will get to shortly.

Here's how the system *could* have evolved, that would have worked better. Teams now have at least six levels of minor league competition, really seven for most teams (AAA, AA, High A, Low A, Rookie, Short-Season Rookie, and international development leagues.) Suppose that we had only four? (A, B, C and D. Which was the original minor league structure, 100 years ago.) Suppose that, rather than running seven or eight minor league teams, big league teams ran 20—two at A level, four at B, six at C, and eight at D.

Of course, it would cost more money to sustain 20 teams than it does to sustain 7 or 8, but this could be and would be offset by other savings. In order to sustain 20 teams on the budget now used for seven, you would have to generate more money from local support for the teams. In order to generate more money from local support, you would have to allow those teams the integrity to conduct a meaningful competition.

What that means, in practice, is that major league teams could not take players away from their minor league subordinates in the middle of the race—something they could not do originally. When free minor league teams made arrangements with major league teams in the 1930s and 1940s, those arrangements always sharply limited the ability of the major league team to move players up in mid-season. A major league team might be able to "move up" one or two players a year during the season—or none; otherwise, they left the roster alone. When a major league team *did* move up a player in mid-season, they were required to replace him with a player from a higher league. This was considered necessary, because how can a minor league team compete, how can they sell their product to their fans, if the interests of the minor league team are openly sacrificed to the interests of the major league team?

After a few years, the minor league operators looked around, and realized that they could not go home again. They could no longer opt out of the arrangements they had entered into, which meant that major league teams could—and did—dictate the terms of the next contract. By the mid-1950s, major league teams generally had the legal right to move players whenever they wanted to move them, but even then—and into the early 1960s—it was considered bad form for a major league team to do this willy-nilly. If a minor league team had a player who was hitting .350 or hitting .300 with power—like Dick Stuart with Lincoln in 1956 or Steve Bilko with Los Angeles in 1956/1957—the major league affiliate was expected to leave him there and let him be the star, let him sell tickets, until the season was over.

By the mid-1960s even this courtesy had become a dead letter. Major league teams moved players up or sent them down whenever and wherever they felt like it, which made it difficult for minor leagues to have meaningful competitions or to sell tickets. If you think about it, the structure I am suggesting here is like the structure of college football or college basketball, in which there are many competitive teams at lower levels, few competitive teams at the highest level, but at any level, professional sports have no ability to invade the team and disrupt the competition in mid-season. Think what it would do the NCAA basketball if the NBA, in mid-season, decided that it liked Kemba Walker or Nolan Smith and would simply sign him to a contract in mid-season, to hell with the NCAA tourney. That's what happened to minor league baseball. The major league teams started taking the best players off the minor league teams in mid-season, which made it impossible for the minor leagues to conduct a meaningful competition.

The major league teams were acting in their selfish best interests, which is a normal thing; all businesses normally do what is best for themselves, rather than worrying about what helps the industry. But by behaving selfishly, major league teams reduced the amount of money flowing into the industry, which placed (essentially) the entire burden of funding the minor league system on the major league teams. Major league teams thus (predictably) cut back on the number of teams in their system. If they had allowed the minor league teams to run legitimate competitions that could sustain fan interest, thus generating income, they could have sustained 20 teams on the money that now goes to eight, but they would all have had to see the point of this at the same time. Enlightened self-interest.

Here's the system I propose—understanding of course that the moment has passed, and in the real world there are sharp limitations on our ability to re-construct what we have...this is the system

I am proposing for a better universe:

a) Two teams at A level, four at B, six at C, eight at D (you said that already).

b) Each league runs a complete season of 150 or more games.

c) Every player going to the major leagues is required to spend three full seasons in the minor leagues, with very limited exceptions.

d) Minor league teams can trade at the *same level* for players who are not on the major league 40-man roster and not under the control of the major league team. Major league teams might be allowed to "control" an additional 25 to 30 players who are not yet on their 40-man roster, as they do in the current system.

e) Minor league teams are not allowed to "trade up" or "trade down" in mid-season.

f) D level teams are allowed to sign new players and release old ones without restraint, but no player from a D level team may be moved to a higher level in mid-season.

g) Some D level teams may be independent operators, unaffiliated with a major league teams.

h) C level teams again could sign players and release them in mid-season, and could "borrow" players from higher leagues for short periods of time with the consent of the higher-level team, but could not accept players promoted in mid-season from D level teams.

i) No more than two players per season could be designated for mid-season advancement from C level to B; however, those players would have to be publicly identified before the start of the season. The players identified would not have to be promoted; however, only those two players could be promoted.

j) B level teams could sign and release players, could borrow players from A level teams for limited periods of time with the consent of those teams, could accept previously designated players promoted in mid-season from C level, and could be forced to give up no more than one player per season to the A level team or the major league team, provided that that player was re-placed by another healthy player who could play the same position.

k) A level teams could sign and release players, and could be forced to give up no more than two players per sea-son (in season) to the major league team, provided that those players were replaced by healthy players coming down from the majors.

Each minor league would have a designated officer—a local fan or a local mayor, for example—who had to consent to a player be-ing loaned to a lower-level team. The idea is that if a minor league team has an injury to a key player when there is a player in the system who is warming the bench at a higher level and who could play regularly for the lower-level team, then the team could "borrow" the higher-ranking player to get them past the injury. But the major league team can't move players up and down just because they feel like it; it has to be done because it works for both minor league teams.

A fourth problem with minor league baseball as it is is that nobody at all cares about the lower-level competitions. If you go to a game in the Gulf Coast League or some of the other low-level leagues, you will notice that there is nobody there. The attendance at the game will consist of wives, girlfriends and parents of the play-ers, a handful of scouts, perhaps ten or fifteen retirees, and that's it; those teams have no fan base whatsoever. It creates a very desultory atmosphere at those games, with the appearance at times that the players are just going through the motions.

I see my system as having the following advantages for major league teams:

1) That it would allow minor league teams to gradually re-build their fan base, thus increasing the amount of revenue flowing into the game,

2) That it would create more opportunities for players with marginal skills but high determination to suc-ceed at the lower levels, thus increasing the flow of talent to the majors,

3) That the three-year mandatory minor league buffer would slightly reduce the pressure on major league teams to pay bonuses to amateur players, and

4) That the three-year minor league buffer and the in-creased regular flow of talent to the majors would sig-

nificantly reduce the pressure on major league teams to do international scouting and to pay high bonuses to international players.

Under the current operating arrangement major league teams are limited as to the number of minor league affiliates they can have. The thinking was that by limiting the number of minor league affiliates MLB would control the costs of operating a minor league system, but this hasn't worked at all; what has happened is that the money that would otherwise have gone into operating a larger minor league system has been diverted into international scouting and international player development. Those costs would not simply go away with a more robust minor league system, but I would predict that they would gradually atrophy, as teams would gradually see more talent rising through their farm systems.

Yes, it would "disadvantage" the major league teams in that they would no longer be able to swap out the major league roster with the triple-A roster in mid-season, as teams do now, but, as it would disadvantage all of the teams in the same manner, it would disadvantage none of them in competition with the others.

In a farm system you would have 20 minor league shortstops—8 at level D, 6 at C, 4 at B, 2 at A, each one of whom had had a full minor league apprenticeship and full seasons at each level of competition. The gap between the highest level of the minors and the majors would shrink back to something more like it was in the 1950s. If you needed a shortstop you would automatically have two candidates to step in. If they were both weak, you'd have 58 trade candidates from the other systems. The fear of being left without a shortstop would diminish as the tide of talent rose.

I would also argue that this system *might*—might possibly—work to depress major league salaries, as it would create more competition for major league jobs, thus driving down marginal salaries. A team now can pay $1.5 million for Jeff Francoeur or whomever because there's a perception that there's nobody else there who can do the job.

Of course, there will be people who will argue that increasing the number of minor league shortstops would not increase the number of *good* shortstops. You only have so many players who have the ability to play in the majors; increasing the number of minor leaguers won't change that. That's a side argument and this isn't the place to get into that, but those people are simply and flatly wrong. Competition produces players. If you increase the number of players who get an opportunity to play, you will increase the number of major-league ready players who come out of the system—not proportionately, but you *will* increase them. If you increase the number of minor league teams by 150%, from 8 to 20, you won't increase the number of major league-ready shortstops by 150%, but you will increase it by 50 or 60%.

More to the point, since talent in baseball is naturally a pyramid, if you make a farm system a pyramid it will produce more players who are able to advance naturally through that system—rather than cutting off opportunity at the lowest level by making premature decisions about who has the "talent" to advance consistently through a tube-shaped system. Talent in the major leagues is the far right-hand side of a bell-shaped distribution curve. If you cut off the right-hand side of a bell-shaped distribution curve and stand it on its side, it's a pyramid.

STOPLIGHTS AND CAMERAS

by Bill James

Has it ever occurred to you that physical stoplights are now completely unnecessary? Visualize an intersection near your home, with stoplights. Now visualize the same intersection as it would look without stoplights. Looks a lot better, right?

Physical stoplights are now totally unnecessary. It would be extremely easy, with modern technology, to have a system that broadcasts stoplight signals directly to the vehicle, where they would be displayed on the dashboard as small red, green and yellow lights. Every vehicle would be required to have working receptors, but with modern technology it's not that big an issue, and there would have to be a small ground-level signal that would tell the pedestrian when it was safe to cross.

I think it would be a better system. I think 95% of people would prefer such a system if they did have it. I think it would be cheaper to operate and cheaper to maintain, and the only reason we don't have it is just the historic pathway of development. The old system was necessary in the past, and we still have it because we don't know how to get rid of it. We don't know where to start. No state can mandate the better system until all the cars have it; the cars don't have it because no state uses it. No state can move until the other states move. It doesn't pay to manufacture the equipment until the system is in place; it doesn't pay to put the system in place until the equipment is manufactured. We're stalemated by the inertia of obsolete technology.

While we are here, I am something of a nut on the subject of red-light cameras. I have been known to rant about red-light cameras until told to shut up.

I think that I was fascinated by the concept, first, as a puzzle. There is something about the idea of being anonymously sent an

$85 ticket for allegedly running a red light that just really chaps my joy buzzer, and I always wish that there was some organization that I could send my $85 to now to fight against these damn things, or, better yet, I wish there was some politician running for Congress who, rather than spending his advertising dollars trying to convince me that the opposing politician is a bigger creep than he is, would spend just a little bit of the money running commercials saying, "Vote for me; I'll introduce legislation to require that any city councilman who proposes installing a red-light camera to be strung up by his testicles, or, if it is a woman, by her toenails." OK, you got my vote. $50 million spent trying to convince me that your opponent is a ne'er-do-well, you're wasting your money; $25 spent opposing red-light cameras, I'm sold.

Another way to defeat them, by the way, is simply to organize and demand a trial. If everybody who hates the cameras demands a trial whenever they get a ticket, that will swamp the system and force it to fail. But why? I mean, it's not like we have a *right* to run red lights, nor is it that I secretly enjoy running red lights, or that I feel entitled to run red lights. I probably haven't had a ticket for running a red light in…I don't know, ten years. Why, then, am I offended by the concept of red light cameras?

Paradoxically, I am all in favor of police public surveillance cameras. Should the police have the right to post video cameras in public areas, to be used to investigate crimes?

Well, hell yes, they should; in fact, I'm in favor of having them pretty much everywhere. What is done in public areas is by definition not "private", and one doesn't have any right to commit crimes without being observed by the police. Put up the cameras everywhere; hell, put one up in my alley. You can use my fence post; I'm all in favor.

OK, well…what's the difference?

We don't want to live in a paranoid country. Americans should not have to drive around in constant fear of straying across an imaginary line. If we have red-light cameras and radar cams, what's next? Lane-straying cameras that send you a ticket when your tire goes out of its lane? Signaling cameras that send you a ticket when you change lanes without signaling? Who wants to live in *that* America?

The thing is, I don't have any *intention* of running red lights. I'm sure that I *do* run red lights from time to time. I'm sure that most everybody does, but it's not done from a desire to break the law or a desire to ignore the law; it sort of just happens. You're in a hurry, you're trying to get out of a traffic box, the light turns yellow, you miscalculate how long it will take you to get through the light and how long the light will stay yellow. It shouldn't cost you $85.

Police surveillance cameras are different because they're not a practical response to petty misbehaviors. A couple of years ago, a guy down my alley had his garage set on fire in the middle of the night. We've had people walk down the alley and spray-paint graffiti. Probably the same people who spray the graffiti are the people who set the fire, but who knows? If you have a surveillance camera, you can review the tapes and maybe identify the people who set the fire. That's deliberate misconduct, intent on causing harm. There is a real need to prevent that.

This relates to a much larger issue. I've just written a book about crime, *Popular Crime*. It is my belief that, in the broad sweep of history, serious crime is being gradually eliminated. You don't see that when you look around you one day at a time. You can't learn that through experience. When you compare America today to America a hundred years ago, when you compare 2010 to 1610, when you compare 1610 to 1010, when you compare 1950 to AD 50, when you compare AD 500 to BC 500, you can see that war, murder, slavery, and other evils are being very gradually eliminated from human history, and that over the period of centuries enormous progress has been made. Not everybody sees that; that's my view.

Over the last hundred years America has made great progress in eliminating murder, and really, it would be in many ways stunningly easy to make vast strides from where we are now. If we could, as a nation, stop the silly left/right arguments and focus on practical solutions, and if we could somehow seize control of the system of justice away from a court system that hampers innovation at every step, we could eliminate 80% of the murders we have now within twenty years. One of the biggest obstacles to that is a barbaric, punishment-based judicial system that has gotten worse over the last 30 years, while many other elements of the system of justice have gotten better.

Punishing people as a way of modifying behavior is massively inefficient at best, and is very often counter-productive. The prison system manufactures as much crime as it prevents. To move forward from where we are now—to move forward rapidly—we have to unhinge the judicial system from the punishment model, and get more focus on repairing the things that are broken. In other words, yes, there are some people who are determined to do wrong, and we have to physically prevent them from doing wrong, but there are many people who stray across the lines because they're not really paying attention to the lines and they're not very good at leading productive lives. These people also need to go to prison; don't get me wrong about that. But they need to be sent to prison and forced to accept help and guidance. Our judicial system too often takes people who just are kind of screwed up and need guidance to live a better life, and pushes them forcefully into the pathways of a criminal life. We need to stop that.

That's a liberal point; there are conservative points that I would make with equal vigor, but you'll have to trust me on that.

We all know why the city councils want red light cameras, don't we? Money. You set up a camera at the right intersection, you can print 200 tickets a day. $85 a ticket, processing costs of $15... what is that, a half-million a year? It's a sweet deal. The companies that manufacture these money-sucking machines are there to assuage your conscience with reassuring studies about how many lives you are saving by preventing people from running red lights. You're doing the right thing, Mr. City Councilman. The fact that you're lining your pockets while doing it is just a side benefit.

The problem is, you're trying to punish people into driving more carefully. It will not work. It will backfire, absolutely and without question. We don't know HOW it will backfire, exactly, but it will. Punishment works through the mechanism of fear. Fear changes people. It makes them angrier. Fear makes people dislike those who cause them to fear.

Look, I obey traffic laws and you obey traffic laws—99% of you—because we wish to be good citizens, we choose to be safe drivers, and we do not intend to violate the laws. Occasionally we may stray; occasionally we may need to be reminded.

It would *more* effective, in preventing accidents and obtaining compliance with traffic laws, if we would *reduce* the number of traffic fines that we levy, and replace the practice of writing costly "tickets" with a system of reminders, feedback and positive re-enforcement designed to keep people focused on voluntary compliance. The problem with the red light cameras is that they risk doing to traffic law enforcement what we have already done with the prison system. It risks creating an ever-expanding cycle of punishment, fear, resistance and evasion.

So here's what we can do with the red-light cameras. I *like* red-light cameras; I support them, I endorse them—under one condition. The one condition is that governments absolutely are not allowed to levy *fines* based on them, or to use them as revenue-producing instruments. If you videotape somebody driving a through a red light, send them a notice, letting them know they've done it. If they do it all the time, if they don't *stop* doing it, even after you call their attention to it...well, that's a different issue.

If it's a $10 fine, OK. If it's no fine if you're caught by a red-light camera but when a policeman writes you a ticket for doing the same thing that adds $50 to the ticket, OK. I don't have a problem with that.

Look, I think the use of technology to expand the capacities of the police force is a good thing. I'm actually in favor of it. What I am opposed to is expanding *punishment* as an instrument of social policy. It is irresponsible to do that. We should be thinking, as a people, about how we can reduce our reliance on a punishment-based justice system, and transition out of that. We certainly should not be rapidly and suddenly expanding it by electronic multiplication.

And if governments are trying to milk money out of essentially good people and essentially careful drivers by electronic snooping, I have a real problem with that, and think it's a very serious issue. It's a big step down the wrong road, when we have an opportunity, because of new technology, to go down a better road, a more productive road.

––··––

Battling Expertise with the Power of Ignorance

by Bill James

———

The first thing that I should say is that I have no credentials whatsoever as a mathematician or a statistician. I have been identified countless times as a statistician, for reasons that I understand, but I have never, ever been *self*-identified as a statistician, for reasons that I will explain. I don't really know anything much about the workings or applications of statistical methods. I could not describe myself as a statistician because I could not meet the standards statisticians would expect a professional statistician to meet. I don't call myself a statistician for the same reason that I don't call myself a plastic surgeon or an auto mechanic: I am afraid that somebody might ask me to tighten their jawline or to fix their Honda, and I wouldn't have a clue how to do it. I have always chosen to call myself a writer because, well, hell, anybody can call himself a writer.

There is more to it than that, actually. Self-definition is dangerous for a public figure, because it indirectly places limits on what one can attempt within the definition. Although I often write about baseball history I don't call myself a historian, either, in part because saying that I am this or that or the other adds limits, but not abilities. If I call myself a historian that doesn't make me any better historian, but am I still allowed to write about the future of the game? If I call myself a statistical analyst am I still allowed to propose theories that have nothing to do with statistics? I have always thought that it was best *not* to define oneself, but to let the world say about you whatever it is that the world chooses to say. This is my first reference point for the Power of Ignorance. By not claiming to know exactly what it is that I am doing, I remain able to attempt whatever it is that I feel like attempting. It's a great advantage.

I should say, unless there be misunderstanding about this, that I am in no way in favor of ignorance or against the advance of knowledge. I have worked my entire life for the advancement of knowledge, trying to increase respect for reason and respect for research in the world of sports. I am embracing ignorance here in this sense and for this reason: that we are all, in my view, condemned to float endlessly in a vast sea of unanswered questions and unknown reference points—a Sea of Ignorance, if you will. The example that I like to use is a chess board. How many moves ahead can you see on a chess board? I can see about one move ahead of myself in a chess game. If you can see 3 or 4 moves ahead on a chess board, you can beat 99% of chess players, and if you could see 7 or 8 moves ahead in a chess game, you would be a world-class chess champion.

Well, suppose that a chess board was not eight squares wide and eight squares long, but a hundred squares wide and a hundred squares long, with a thousand moving pieces, rather than 32. How far ahead could you see on a chess board then? The world is like a chess board that is a million squares wide and a million squares long with hundreds of thousands of moving pieces and hundreds of thousands of different players moving them. In my view, anyone who imagines that he can anticipate what will happen next, in any area of life, is delusional, and people who think that experts *should* be able to do this are children and fools.

If the world was 10% more complicated than the human mind, or even if it was 40% more complicated or ten times more complicated, then the difference between an intelligent person's ability to understand the world and a less intelligent person's ability to understand the world would be very meaningful. But since the world is billions and billions of times more complicated than the human mind, individual intelligence is almost entirely irrelevant to the understanding of the world. What is critical to understanding is humility and cooperation. What is critical to gaining more understanding of the world is to learn to accept and appreciate the vastness of our ignorance, and to understand that one can only survive in a sea of ignorance by working with others to make our small lifeboat a little bit stronger. Only by embracing the fact of our limitless ignorance can one position oneself to increase the store of knowledge.

———·———

The way that baseball was understood 35 years ago, and the way that it is understood today, is largely by the interpretations of experts. I don't in any way want to speak disrespectfully of experts, but experts are people who claim to know things, and who claim to understand how something works. There are a vast number of things that the experts all knew 35 years ago, based on their experience in the game and based on their education by others, older than themselves. The experts all knew, for example, that the prime of a player's career was ages 28 to 32. The experts all knew that when there was a runner on first and no one out, the percentage move was to bunt. The experts all knew that speed was tremendously important, and that the difference between good teams and bad teams was mostly in how they performed in clutch situations. The experts all knew that a good starting pitcher would draw a few thousand extra fans to the game every time he took the mound.

Through 1970, through 1975, there was essentially no one in the world who was in the habit of submitting these axioms of expertise to objective test. When I began writing about baseball in 1975, the first thing I did was to say, "Well, I don't know anything. I'm not an expert. But perhaps I could contribute to the conversation by finding a way to take these things that the experts know, and look to see, as best I can, whether they are objectively true."

If you want to know who I am and what I have done for a living for the last 35 years, I can explain it in one sentence. My job is to find questions about baseball that have objective answers. That is all that I do; that is basically all that I have done for the last 35 years. I listen carefully to what is said to be true about baseball, and I try to find elements in those claims which are capable of objective answer. For example, when it was suggested that baseball players peaked from ages 28 to 32, we (that is, me and a few others who eventually came to be called "sabermetricians" after The Society for the Advancement of Baseball Research) asked, "OK, do players hit more home runs at ages 28 to 32 than at other ages? How many home runs are hit by players at age 27? At age 22? At every other age? How many doubles are hit, how many games do pitchers win at each age, how many strikeouts do they record, etc.?

It turned out in this case that what the experts all knew to be true—that baseball players are in their prime from ages 28 to 32—is just totally, wildly and complete untrue. It doesn't match the data in any way, shape or form. 27-year-old players hit 68% more home runs in the major leagues than do 32 year-old players—thus, saying that 32-year-old players are in their prime and 27-year-old players are not is preposterous.

When you formulate a question which has an objective answer and you go and find that answer, you almost always wind up with a set of numbers. "Numbers", in baseball, are usually referred to as "statistics", even if they are not the kind of numbers that would ordinarily be described as "statistics" in any other area of life. Because the questions that I asked led to the formation of new statistics, I became known as a statistician.

It is quite astonishing to me, in retrospect, that no one before me had tried to make a living by doing this. There was a large community of baseball experts who worked for baseball teams and wrote about baseball, based on this large, shared body of "expertise". A very, very large percentage of the things that the experts all knew to be true turned out, on examination, to be not true at all. It is not true that bunting increases either the number of runs that are scored or the expectation of scoring a single run. It is not true that speed is a key element of successful baseball teams, clutch hitting is either 99 or 100% a chimera, and the identity of the starting pitcher has, except in a very few cases, no detectable impact on the attendance at a game. I'll deal with a couple of these claims in more detail later on, but when I began to publish articles and later books reporting on research which demonstrated that some of the claims of experts were demonstrably false, this put me at loggerheads with the baseball establishment. There was, in the first fifteen years of my career, a great deal of misunderstanding about what I was doing. People thought—and, indeed, some people still think—that I was trying to supplant the experts, and become an expert myself. Some people thought that I was anti-expert, or anti-scout. This was never true. In fact, I have always had great respect and great admiration for the scouts. There are a large number of things about baseball that I have no way of studying…no way of knowing based on the records. I admire the ability of scouts to look at a young hitter, and note things about his swing that may predict whether he will be able to adjust to higher levels of competition. Having sat next to scouts at hundreds of major league baseball games, I am always astonished by the things that they can see that I would never have seen in a million years had someone not pointed them out to me. I also admire, and lust after, those really cool radar guns. The only thing is, everything the scouts say is not the gospel truth.

———————

In my early career, people would attack me by pointing out that I had no credentials to be considered an expert. I fell into the habit of saying, "That's right; I don't."

I want to point out to you in passing that "getting the answers right" had almost nothing to do with the success of my career. My reputation is based entirely on finding the right questions to ask—that is, in finding questions that have objective answers, but to which no one happens to know what the objective answer is. That's what I did 35 years ago; that's what I do now. When I do that, it makes almost no difference whether I get the answer right, or whether I get it a little bit wrong. Of course I do my very best to get the answers right, out of pride and caution, but it doesn't actually matter.

Why?

Because if I don't get the answer right, somebody else will. It is called "science."

Again, I am not qualified to lecture anyone about the scientific method. In fact, my understanding of the scientific method is very rudimentary, very primitive. Nonetheless, the scientific method has been the greatest ally of my career. Basically, what I know about the scientific method would fit onto a bumper sticker, and, that being the case, I might as well read you the bumper sticker. Scientists design tests to see whether an assertion is compatible or incompatible with the evidence. When they do that, someone else will always figure out some way to do another test, and a better test. When that happens, it is the scientist' responsibility to acknowledge that the other person's research is better than his or is an advancement from his. What is necessary to the advancement of knowledge, then, is humility—the capacity to recognize that other people have accomplished something that we have not been able to accomplish. That, then, is the bumper sticker: "What is necessary to the advancement of knowledge is humility."

When you go to an expert and you say, "I don't think what you are saying is true," that will be perceived as arrogance. Who are you to challenge the experts? But it is not arrogance, at all; it is grounded in the understanding that we are all floating in a vast sea of ignorance, and that much of what we all believe to be true will later be shown to be nonsense. To recognize this is not arrogance; it is humility.

When I was in Elementary School in the early 1960s, our principal was fond of telling us that, when he was a young man just after World War One, he took a college chemistry class in which the professor told the students that they were studying science at the ideal time, because all of the important discoveries had been made now. Everything that there was to be known about chemistry or biology or physics, he suggested, was pretty much known by then.

———————

As I said, I call the search for objective knowledge about baseball "sabermetrics", and you would be amazed how common it is for us to hear that everything worthwhile to be known about sabermetrics is known now, and everybody who cares about it knows it. In reality, nothing has changed, at all; all we have done is to take a few buckets of water out of the ocean of ignorance and move them over into the small pond of real knowledge. In reality, the ocean of ignorance is larger than it ever was, as it expands on its own.

Baseball teams play 162 games a year. I just realized last week that, sometime in the last 20 years, baseball experts have fallen into the habit of saying that a baseball team has about 50 games a year that you are just going to lose no matter what, 50 games a year that you're going to win, and it is the other 62 games that determine what kind of season you're going to have. A more inane analysis would be difficult to conceive of. First of all, baseball teams do not play one hundred non-competitive games a year, or anything remotely like that. Baseball teams play about forty non-competitive games in a season, more or less; I would be surprised if any team in the history of major league baseball ever had a hundred games in the season that were just wins or losses, which the losing team never had a chance to win after the fourth or fifth inning. The outcome of *most* baseball games, in fact, could be reversed by changing a very small number of events within the game.

But setting that aside, this relatively new cliché assumes that it is the outcome of the most competitive games that decides whether a team has a great season or a poor season. In reality, the opposite is true. The more competitive a game is, the more likely it is that the game will be won by the weaker team. If the Royals play the Yankees and the score of the game is 12 to 1, it is extremely likely that the Yankees won. If the score is 4 to 3, it's pretty much a tossup. The reasons why this is true will be intuitively obvious to those of you who work with statistics for a living. It is the *non*-competitive games—the blowouts—that play the largest role in determining what kind of season a team has. Misinformation about baseball continues to propagate, and will continue to propagate forever more, without regard to the fact that there is now a community of researchers that studies these things.

One of the most enduring debates about the applications of statistical analysis to baseball has to do with the role of speed on a successful team. Speed in baseball is tied more closely to stolen bases than to any other statistical category. By the late 1970s, we had studied the statistics of successful and unsuccessful baseball teams to such an extent that we could place values on each event. The statistics of baseball teams predict runs scored so reliably that is extremely easy to see that teams that hit 150 home runs score more runs than teams that hit 140 home runs. It is easy to see that teams that hit 240 doubles score more runs than teams that hit 230 doubles, and that teams that hit 230 doubles score more runs than teams that hit 220 doubles. It is easy to see, in the records of baseball, that teams that draw 550 walks in a season score more runs than teams that draw 540 walks. The end result of each isolated event is easy to see in the overall mix, so much so that it is very easy to place a value on one walk, one single, one double, one triple or one home run.

The only exception to this is that the effect of stolen bases appear to be nearly invisible. Teams that steal bases not only don't score *more* runs than teams that don't steal bases, they actually score slightly fewer runs—or at least they did 35 years ago.

Obviously, stolen bases can correlate negatively with runs scored because stolen base attempts can lead either to stolen bases, which are positive, or to runners caught stealing, which are negative. By contrasting the value of a stolen base with the cost of a runner caught stealing, one can calculate what success percentage is needed to break even. It turns out that through much of baseball history, teams were attempting to steal bases at a success rate that was actually causing them to score fewer runs than if they had not attempted to steal any bases at all. Our capacity to misunderstand the world is almost without limit. In recent decades this negative effect of stealing bases has not been true, but even in modern baseball, the actual success rate is so close to the break even percentage that the runners caught stealing eat up almost all of the value of the stolen base attempts, so that the gain in runs per stolen base attempt is along the lines of one run per 25 attempts. Stolen bases are essentially irrelevant to successful offenses. If a baseball team can add a player who hits five extra doubles or a player who steals 50 extra bases, they're usually better off to add the player who hits a handful of doubles.

There are many other ways that one can study the value of a stolen base. We can calculate the inherent run value—that is, the probable runs scored—when there is a runner on first, no one out, and when there is a runner on second, no one out, etc.

One can create simulations of baseball offenses in which we generate random sequences of events with and without stolen base attempts, and see what the change in runs resulting is when the stolen base attempts are added.

One can evaluate the stolen base attempt with a Markov Chain analysis. . .that is, real statiticians may be able to do this; I can't, but many other people have.

The thing is that no matter which one of these approaches one takes, one always comes back with the conclusion that stolen bases are essentially irrelevant to a successful offense. Of course, this does not prove that speed is not important or that speed is not tremendously valuable; it merely demonstrates that stolen base attempts are relatively insignificant. Speed is not the same as "stolen bases".

When I published research questioning the value of speed in the late 1970s—and other researchers did as well—we were confronted by a barrage of arguments from the experts offering a hundred different reasons why we had to be wrong. This was entirely appropriate. It is not the scientific method that when somebody publishes a few studies concluding that X is untrue, everybody accepts that X is untrue, and stops asserting X. There are a wide variety of reasons why speed could be important, even though stolen bases were not. It could be, for example, that the value of stolen bases was hidden by a cross-correlation—that is, that as teams got better hitters they had less need to steal bases, thus bad teams stole more bases than good teams, even though the steals themselves were a positive. Well, yes, that's true, but it's also pretty easy to remove the cross-correlation and study the stolen bases of teams that are otherwise similar, and the conclusion remains that stolen bases tend not to be closely associated with good teams.

One can study the question of speed without looking at stolen bases by looking at other categories of performance that tend to be dependent on speed, such as triples and grounding into double plays, but that leads to the same conclusion: there is little or no evidence that fast teams tend to be good teams.

One thing that I would hear often, and still hear sometimes, is that the value of speed is that it prevents double plays. But the value of the stolen base attempt in preventing double plays is accounted for in many or all of the approaches that have already been outlined, so this argument is essentially simply a misunderstanding of how the conclusion was reached.

The central question of analytical research in baseball is "why do teams win?" What are the actual characteristics of winning teams? The rest of baseball analysis consists mostly of breaking that question down into a thousand smaller questions. The most damning fact for speed teams is that there is essentially no correlation between speed and wins. You can say anything you want to about why speed is important in baseball, but all this accomplishes logically is to make the mystery deeper. If there are all of these advantages to speed in baseball, then why don't speed teams win? The fact remains that they don't, but let's move on to another issue.

Our work can be divided into two areas. One is efforts to answer the question, "What is the relationship between X and Y?", and the other is efforts to answer the question "How can we measure that?" The first half of my career was largely devoted to efforts to state in simple formulas the relationships between different things in baseball—the relationship between runs scored and wins, for example, or the relationship between the different types of hit elements and runs scored. I developed in the years from 1975 to 1990 a large number of heuristic rules for addressing various problems in baseball research. The two best known of these are the Pythagorean theory of runs to wins, and the Runs Created formula.

The Pythagorean theory of runs to wins, which I first published in 1977, states that the ratio between a team's wins and losses will be the same as the relationship between the square of their runs scored and square of their runs allowed. In other words, if a team scored four runs a game on average and allowed three runs a game, their winning percentage would be about .640, or a ratio of sixteen to nine. Later research has demonstrated that the Pythagorean theory works better with an exponent other than 2.00, and still later research has demonstrated that it works better still if you modify the exponent for the level of scoring. Still, those modifications give only tiny gains in accuracy, and the Pythagorean theory is now almost universally understood and is widely accepted in baseball.

The other heuristic of mine that a lot of people know is the Runs Created formula, which states that the number of runs that a team will score can be predicted by the formula: hits plus walks, times total bases, divided by (at bats plus walks). I introduced this formula in 1978. The essential question about a hitter is not how many hits he gets, or what his on base percentage is, or his slugging percentage, but how many runs he puts on the scoreboard. I thus looked for two or three years for the simplest way to estimate how many runs each player had produced, and this was it. There are now dozens of variations of the Runs Created formula in use, but the simple one from 1978 still works fine. In 2009, 27 of the 30 teams came within seven games of winning the number of games predicted by the 1977 version of the Pythagorean theory, and 26 of 30 teams came within 5% of scoring the number of runs predicted by the 1978 version of the Runs Created formula.

I developed a lot of other heuristics in those years, many of which still survive, like the Power/Speed Number, Secondary Average, Game Scores, Similarity Scores, and something I called the Favorite Toy. The Favorite Toy is a way of estimating the chance that a player will get 3,000 career hits or hit 500 home runs or reach some such goal. The method is so crude and so arbitrary that, at the time I developed it in the early 1970s, I was certain that I would figure out some better way to do this within a few weeks. It's been almost 40 years, and I never have; the spooky thing about that stupid little formula is that it insists on working, although there are a dozen obvious reasons why it shouldn't.

———

In the second half of my career, what I have done more of is to figure out ways to define and measure things that people talk about, but which aren't measured because nobody has taken the trouble to figure out how to measure them. Much of this research is more or less parallel to what a surveyor does. You know what a surveyor does? He puts a post in the ground and measures everything from where the post was. At some point people forget that the starting point of the measurement was entirely arbitrary, and begin to accept the relative nature of the measurements.

Baseball announcers and experts often use terms that have no exact definition, like "manufactured run". A manufactured run, more or less, is a run that a team scores by putting little parts of a run together, like a walk, a stolen base, a ground out and a single. A walk and a single don't add up to a run, but when you add in the stolen base and the ground ball moving up the runner, you get a run out of it. That's a manufactured run.

There is a sort of general agreement about what is a manufactured run, but there is no data because there is no precise operational definition. My contribution to this discussion has been to make up a specific operational definition that says what is and what is not a manufactured run. I did this about four years ago, and, to this point, my definition has had no impact whatsoever on the discussion. But that's just because, at this time, we haven't yet reached the point at which people have stopped focusing on the arbitrary nature of the starting point.

I didn't make up the definition of a manufactured run out of whole cloth. What I did was, I listened very carefully to what people were saying, identifying the occasions on which people would use the term "manufactured run". Then I looked back at what had happened, and tried to identify the circumstances that caused people to use the term. I am not saying that I got it *exactly* right. Perhaps I got it 80% right, perhaps less. But I am saying that, in the long run, people will accept the definition and begin to use the data, simply because a concept is much more useful when it has a specific definition than when it does not.

A great deal of my work over the second half of my career has been to replace free-floating concepts with specific definitions—for example, I've made up specific definitions for "bombs"—that is to say, when an intentional walk blows up on a manager. It's a common expression; it merely occurred to me one day to ask "What exactly does that mean?" Once you realize that you don't know, then you can write a definition, then you can produce data based on the definition, then you can study the issue.

Once the data is produced, of course, it becomes a "statistic", and I become known as the person who has invented yet another new statistic. But is writing definitions really the work of a statistician? I'll leave that up to you. Call me whatever you want to call me.

Probably the most useful thing that I have ever devised, in terms of practical value to real baseball teams, is Similarity Scores. Similarity Scores consist of an entirely arbitrary set of values used to measure the differences between any two players—so arbitrary, in fact, that I usually choose to re-invent them every time I use them, rather than sticking with any set of values.

But Similarity Scores are tremendously useful because, in order to study anything in baseball, you need to identify similar players or similar teams. If you want to know how much money a player should be paid, the first thing you look at is how much money is paid to similar players. If you are trying to figure out how long a player might last, how many years he has left, the most useful way to study the issue is to identify similar players, and study what happened to them. If a player has a very poor year, and you are trying to figure out what his chances are of snapping back, it is very useful to be able to find similar players who had bad years at a similar point in their career. Although it is grounded in nothing—"similarity" is an entirely subjective concept—the method turns out to be of ubiquitous value to real baseball teams facing real life issues.

But everything depends upon recognizing what you do not know, and this gets back to the Power of Ignorance. The great mistake that analysts make is that we always want to focus on what we DO know; we want to make inferences based on what we have studied in the past. We like to do that because, like everyone else, we are trying to purchase credibility based on the work we have done.

But the problem is, you don't learn anything by focusing on the stuff that you already know. In order to expand the sphere of what is known about baseball, you have to find a question that has an answer, but you don't know what the answer is. In other words, you have to learn to identify your own ignorance. You have to get comfortable with ignorance; you have to learn to embrace your ignorance. By doing so, you acquire the ability to expand knowledge.

If you take a bad baseball team, a team that makes bad decisions, and you ask, "Why do they do this?" it will never be ignorance that is the culprit. The problem is not what teams do not know. The problem is what they do know that isn't true.

I have spent my career battling experts, working with the raw material of ignorance. This has always worked for me, because ignorance is an inexhaustible resource. We are all so desperate to understand the world that we manufacture misunderstandings by the yard. Creating knowledge to combat ignorance...creating tools with which to study something...these are slow and time-consuming activities. Making superstitious connections is quick and easy. That sounds judgmental and it shouldn't. The reality is that we're not capable of understanding the world, because the world is vastly more complicated than the human mind. I don't know if that is a complete explanation of myself or not, but it's the best I can do.

———·——

(Note: This is a re-edited version of a speech that was delivered to the Kansas University Statistics Department in 2010.)

This article is reprinted here as it appeared in the *1983 Baseball Abstract*.
At the conclusion of the article I'll have a series of other comments.

THE LAW OF COMPETITIVE BALANCE

by Bill James

————

Several years ago I undertook a series of studies which were designed to enable me to predict the movement of a team upward or downward in one year based on an analysis of several factors from the year before – a subject, it happens, which no longer interests me. I was attempting, by finding the answers to a series of relevant questions, to develop a sort of "technical analysis" of the season to come. Those questions included:

What percentage of the time does a team improve in one season if its starting lineup in the previous season averages 25 years of age? Or 26, 27, 28,...33?

If a team improves in one season, what percentage of the time will they also improve in the next?

What is the average win total in the next season of teams which win 100 games in one season? Teams that win 70 games? 90?

Do teams which change managers usually improve?

I eventually concluded, to complete the digression, that while there was knowledge to be gained by answering the questions, the subject was...how shall I say? Beyond the capacities of the research. A lot of fans feel that your ability to predict the pennant race is a test of your expertise as an analyst. My feeling is that nobody in the world can predict a pennant race, period, because the outcome is dependent on major variables of which no knowledge can exist at the time the prediction must be made. And to the very limited extent that a race is predictable, I think you'd have better luck with systematic fundamental analysis, as Pete Palmer has, than with the technical analysis that I was trying to develop.

But some of the answers to these questions remain interesting:

1) What I have since described as the Plexiglass Principle: If a team improves in one season, it will likely decline in the next.
2) Now called the Whirlpool Principle: All teams are drawn forcefully toward the center. Most of the teams which had winning records in 1982 will decline in 1983; most of the teams which had losing records in 1982 will improve in 1983.

Other studies later extended both of these principles to individuals. If a player's batting average improved in one season, I found, it would likely decline in the next, and vice versa. The players who hit for the highest averages in one season, I found, would reliably decline in the next season. Of those who hit for the lowest averages, most would not be playing regularly in the following season, but most of those who were playing regularly would raise their batting averages.

There was also an odd similarity in the percentages of improvement and decline, which we will call the 70/50 rule. About 70% of all teams which improve in one year will decline in the next; about 70% of the declines will then improve. Also, 70% of winning teams decline, and 70% of losing teams improve. The same percentages apply to players. In all cases, the amount of overall decline or improvement is about 50%; that is, teams which finish 20 games over .500 in Year I will finish an average about 10 games over in Year II, players who improved their batting averages by 30 points in Year I would decline by 15 points in Year II.*

Why does this happen?

These were not things that I had expected to find. Weaned on the notion of "momentum" since childhood, I had expected a team which won 83 games one year and 87 the next to continue to improve, to move on to 90; instead, they consistently relapsed. Half-expecting to find that the rich grow richer and the poor grow poorer, I found instead that the rich and the poor converged on a common

---

*For the sake of clarity, the 70/50 rule does not apply uniformly regardless of distance from .500, or regardless of previous movement. If you're talking about a team which is 40 games over .500 or a batter whose average improves 75 points, the chance of a decline is over 90%, which if you are talking about an 82-80 team or a player whose average is up 5 points, it is barely over 50%.

target at an alarming rate of speed. Sporting teams behave over a period of years as if a powerful magnetic center was drawing on them, tugging them toward it, defying them to stay up or to stay down or to drift away from it.

Why does this happen, and how does it happen? The Law of Competitive Balance: There develop over time separate and unequal strategies adopted by winners and losers; the balance of those strategies favors the losers, and thus serves constantly to narrow the difference between the two. There develop (in all sports and in life in general—it is merely that the orderliness and detailed record-keeping of the games of life enables us to trace its effects more clearly in the sporting world) over-time (within a season, between seasons, within a game, between games) separate and unequal strategies which are adopted by winners and losers (and which logically should be adopted by winners and losers). The balance of those strategies always favors the team which is behind, and thus serves constantly to narrow the difference between the two (between the team which is behind in a game and the team which is ahead, between the team which has been strong and the team which has been weak).

The essence of the difference is in how the two teams view the need to make changes. If a team wins 96 games and its division, that team develops a self-satisfaction which colors all of the decisions that the team needs to face. The team looks over its roster and discovers, say, a 31-year old shortstop coming off a .238 season. If the team had finished out of contention, there is little doubt that they would replace that player. As a bad team, what they would likely do is look for a kid with ability, somebody who might play the position for them for 10 or 12 years. As a near-miss contender, what they would do is look for a proven player who could help them get over the hump. But as a winner there is a tendency to say "Well, he's only 31, he's had some good years, and he's still doing the job on defense. We won the pennant with him last year." And thus the winning team, because they are winners, does not address the problem.

I did a little study to demonstrate that this really does happen. What I did was to take all of the teams since the 162-game schedule was adopted which have won 90 to 96 games (except in the strike-shortened 1972 season). About each of them I asked four things:

1) Did they win the pennant or division?
2) How many of the same eight regulars returned as regulars in the following season?
3) How many games did the team win in the following season?
4) Did the team win its league or division in the following season?

The 90-96 group was chosen because it contains both winners and non-winners. Actually, the study covered 18 of the former and 40 of the losers. Those two groups of teams when compared in the first season were nearly identical in all categories of performance except "finish." The "winners" group averaged 92.3 wins, 714 runs scored and a .5705 won-lost percentage. The losers averaged 92.1 wins, 706 runs scored and a .5698 won-lost percentage. But in the following seasons:

1) The winners returned 81% of the same regulars to the starting lineup (116 of 144 players), the losers only 75% (241 of 320).
2) The won-lost percentages of both groups declined in the following seasons, but while the winners declined to an aggregate .536 won-lost percentage, the losers held up to .549.
3) Twelve of the 40 "losers" won the pennant or division in the following season, or 30%. Only three of the 18 "winners" did the same.

Exactly the effects that the Law of Competitive Balance would predict. It would predict many others which I haven't checked out. For example, if you studied the replacement rates for players hitting .220-.229, .230-.239, .240-.249 and .250-.259, you should find that a regular player who hits, let's say, a .236, is more likely to be replaced if he plays on a team which wins 70 games than if he plays on a team which wins 80, is more likely to be replaced on a team which wins 80 games than on a team which wins 85, more likely on 85 than 90, and more likely on a team which wins 90 and finishes second than on a team which wins 90 and wins the pennant. Below 70…well, you might get into a range there where a .236 hitter is one of the team's stars.

In other sports more than in baseball this process of adaptation takes place inside the game. In a basketball game, if one team runs off a string of points, which team calls time? Review the situation in your mind: Notre Dame leads Grunt State 33-28 with 8 minutes left in the first half. Suddenly, Grunt State rips off nine quick points; it is 37-33 with five left in the half. Who calls time out? Obviously, Notre Dame. What does the announcer say? "Only a four point lead in the first half, but Grunt State really has the momentum going for them now." But what actually happens, in your experience, when the teams come out of the meeting? Does Grunt State go into the half with a 10-point lead? Never happen. Notre Dame will come out and restore order 9½ times in 10.

Why? Because, who changes his strategy? Who runs in a substitute? The Notre Dame coach says "Hey, they're beating us bad on the boards and killing us on the outlet. John, you've got to get up over the back of that Moose; I put Wilson in to get back and head off the break." But what can the Grunt State coach do? He is frozen by his success. The operating dynamic in the situation is not the "momentum" that the announcer will be talking about; it is the Law of Competitive Balance.

A beautiful example of the Law of Competitive Balance occurs in football, with respect to what is called the Nickle Defense: The Nickle Defense involves the use of an extra—a fifth—defensive back, a move which makes it easier to move the ball on the ground (the line is short a man) but more difficult to throw a long pass. Most fans hate the thing; the call-in shows are full of it. "Why do they use that thing? How often do you see a team hold its opponent in check all game, get a lead late and go to that Nickle Defense and allow the other team to march right down the field and get back into the game." In a narrow sense, they're right—it does happen. A lot. But what people don't understand is that when a team gets behind, say 12 points behind in the middle of the fourth quarter, they become increasingly willing to gamble. They might have a long pass play in their book which they figure has maybe a 30% chance of being a long gainer, a 5% chance of being a touchdown, but a 15% chance of being intercepted. Now, in a close game you're not going to use that play except on 3rd and long; it helps your opponent more than it helps you. But if you're two touchdowns behind with time running out, you go to it. It doesn't make any difference if you lose by two touchdowns or three; a play that improves your chances of winning from 15% to 18% is worth running. If your chances of winning are 50%, a 30% gamble looks bad; if they are 15%, it looks great.

It is worth running, and it is worth defending against. If you don't use the Nickle Defense, you're giving them the 15% to 18% improvement; if you do, you're letting them march downfield on the ground.

What the fan is observing when he sees the late rally is not the effect of the Nickle Defense, at all; it is the effect of the Law of Competitive Balance. Teams which have been held in check all game are going to score late sometimes, regardless of what defense you use, because they gain a strategic advantage from being behind.

There is a very similar defensive maneuver that takes place in baseball—except, being baseball, it happens in a much more subtle way. You know the saying about guarding the lines in the late innings of a close game? Why do they do that?

To move the third baseman nearer the line decreases the chance that a ball will be hit safely down the line, but increases the chance that a ball will be hit between third and short. Thus it *increases* the chance of a single, but *decreases* the chance of a double. The move generally allows more singles than it prevents doubles, thus it *increases* the chance that the opposition will be able to put together a big inning. But, because it prevents the double which would put the runner in scoring position, it *decreases* the chance of allowing a single run. Announcers like to puzzle over why you guard the lines in the late innings when you don't early. You guard the lines in late innings when you wouldn't early for exactly the same reason that you bunt in the late innings or issue an intentional walk in the late innings. Baseball is a big-inning game; in the third inning, the key thing is not to give up those three- or four-run innings that will blow you out. But in the 8th inning, it doesn't matter whether you lose by one or three. The one-run inning becomes much more important, so you guard the line.

Plunging on into what is now a full-fledged digression....

I am convinced that the rule of thumb about guarding the lines in the late innings of a close game is on balance a good one. It has evolved through the Natural Selection of Strategies; it has stood the test of time. However, I am much less sure that it is a good one *in all parks*. It is very possible that there are parks, like Royals Stadium and Three Rivers and Busch, where the danger of a double down the line should *always* take precedence, from the first inning on, and it could well be that there are parks, like Dodger Stadium, where the grass slows the ball down to where it is never that grave of a threat, and in which, therefore, one should not guard the lines in the late innings. How long would it take you to come to that realization just by watching?

In the first stages of free agency, many people believed that free agency would enable the rich to grow richer while the poor grew poorer. Of course, just the opposite has happened—the standard deviation of wins has declined from 12.3 in 1978 to 11.6 in 1980 and 10.5 in 1982. Fourteen teams were within 5½ games of first place on September 15, 1982, and if that isn't a record it sure isn't a symptom of ailing competitive balance. George Foster said last year, and was widely quoted as saying, that we would never again see superteams like the 1975-1976 Reds; with free agency, he said, nobody could afford them. What people are saying about free agency now, we should note, is *exactly the opposite* of what they originally said. Then they said it would *destroy* competitive balance; now, it is going to *enforce* competitive balance.

Why has that happened? For a lot of reasons, but what it comes down to is the Law of Competitive Advantage. How many players have actually left weak teams to go join contenders? Damn few. A lot of the strong teams—the Dodgers, the Royals, the Reds—began by turning up their noses at free agency. They could afford to. The St. Louis Cardinals may have wanted Floyd Bannister, but when it comes right down to it, did they want him as much as the cities that didn't already *have* a World Champion? Of the four early big spenders in the free agent market, three—the Angels, Braves and Padres—were poor teams trying to buy championships. The more help you need, the more seriously you look at the options that can help you. The more fluid talent is (the more free is its movement from team to team), the greater competitive balance there will be.

Incidentally, this song about the rich getting richer and the poor getting poorer has been sung many times before. For example, when the roster limits were raised to 25 men, people said that this would enable the strong teams to stockpile talent and keep players who could play for other teams sitting on the Yankees' bench. But as the chart below shows, competitive balance in fact has grown steadily throughout the century, leading now to the virtual disappearance of the .650 baseball team:

Years	Standard Deviation of Won-Lost Percentage	Percentage of Teams Finishing Within Ten Games of First Place
1900-1904	.102	33%
1910-1914	.100	18%
1920-1024	.087	34%
1090-1934	.098	30%
1940-1944	.094	24%
1950-1954	.093	32%
1960-1964	.087	32%
1970-1974	.069	41%

Another place where the Law of Competitive Balance can be observed statistically is in World Series play, by breaking down the won/lost sequences. Who usually wins the second game of the World Series, the team which won the first game and thus leads 1-0, or the team which is behind 1-0? The team which has lost the first game of the series will win the second game 56% of the time (44-35 in 79 World Series). If the series is 2-1 after three games, who usually wins the fourth? Again, over half (52%, 33 of 63) have been won by the teams which were behind. If it is 3-2 after five games, who usually wins the sixth? The teams training 3-2 have won 62% of the time in those games, 28 of 45.

Why? Because they adjust. Who moved his infielder in a couple of steps after the first game of the 1982 Series? Look at the lineups for the first two games of the series:

Milwaukee	
First	Second
Molitor	Molitor
Yount	Yount
Cooper	Cooper
Simmons	Simmons
Oglivie	Oglivie
Thomas	Thomas
Howell	Howell
Moore	Moore
Gantner	Gantner

St. Louis	
First	Second
Herr	Herr
L. Smith	Oberkfell
Hernandez	Hernandez
Hendrick	Hendrick
Tenace	Porter
Porter	L. Smith
Green	Iorg
Oberkfell	McGee
O. Smith	O. Smith

Granted, Milwaukee switched from a lefthander to a righthander, and granted, Herzog switches his lineup around a lot more than Kuenn. But I would bet dollars to pesos that if you checked, you would find that teams *losing* the first game of a World Series make far more lineup changes than teams *winning* the first game. You lose the first game, you start wondering, do we have enough power to win in this park? Could we take more advantage of the bunt with their third baseman? Is our first baseman ever going to come out of his slump? You win the first game, and you make excuses for the first baseman.

A team which *loses* a pennant by three games or less is much more likely to win the race in the following season than is a team which wins by three or less. Again, an observable fact, which the Law of Competitive Balance explains.

The Law of Competitive Balance also applies to individuals. Who experiments with a new batting stroke, a .300 hitter, or a guy who is fighting to keep his job? Who tries to develop a new slider, an 18-game winner or a guy fighting to stay in the big leagues? The less talent you have, the more you are forced to learn, to adapt, to adjust. Among the ten best managers in baseball today, who was more than a marginal player? This process constantly diminishes the distance between the best players and the worst; it draws the George Bretts and Dennis Eckersleys down and it lifts the Brian Downings and the Charlies Houghs up.

And finally, it defines greatness. It is true in all sports, but it is more true in baseball than in others: Greatness in an athlete is self-defined. Great ballplayers in baseball are those who erect standards for themselves so that they redefine an 18-13 season as a failure and only a hard 20 as a success. Great ballplayers continue to experiment, continue to try things, continue to learn before they are on the road to oblivion. What does Pete Rose talk about when he talks about hitting? Adjustments: move up in the box, move back in the box; choke up on the bat, go down to the knob. He is talking about not letting them drag you down. He is talking about what you have to do to defy the Law of Competitive Balance.

NOTES ADDED IN 2011:

1) Early in this article we pose the question, why do teams which are strong tend to grow weaker, and why do teams which are weak tend to grow stronger:

> *Why does this happen, and how does it happen? The Law of Competitive Balance: There develop over time separate and unequal strategies adopted by winners and losers; the balance of those strategies favors the losers, and thus serves constantly to narrow the difference between the two.*

I have no doubt, 28 years later, that the "separate and unequal strategies" distinction that I drew here is real, and I could cite now many, many more studies in which this has been evident. However, the tendency of teams to move toward the center is caused by this phenomenon *and by many other causes.* I should have been more clear about that.

2) My argument about free agency and competitive balance turned out, in retrospect, to be incorrect in the long run. It may have been true in the short run that free agency interacted with the law of competitive balance to decrease the difference between the best teams and the weakest, but in the long run it certainly was *not* true. I was on the wrong side of that issue.

3) This statement is, I believe, historically incorrect:

> *When the roster limits were raised to 25 men, people said that this would enable the strong teams to stockpile talent and keep players who could play for other teams sitting on the Yankees' bench.*

I think when I wrote that I was confusing the beginning of the 25-man roster—which occurred in 1917 or 1918—with efforts that were made in the late 1930s to prevent the Yankees and Cardinals from stockpiling minor league talent. There were several efforts made in the late 1930s to diminish the dominance of the Yankees, but this had nothing to do with the 25-man roster limit.

4) I re-calculated the standard deviations of winning percentages given in this chart:

Years	Standard Deviation of Won-Lost Percentage	Percentage of Teams Finishing Within Ten Games of First Place
1900-1904	.102	33%
1910-1914	.100	18%
1920-1024	.087	34%
1090-1934	.098	30%
1940-1944	.094	24%
1950-1954	.093	32%
1960-1964	.087	32%
1970-1974	.069	41%

I re-calculated all of those percentages, and I come up with the following notes or problems. For the years 1910-1914, I get a standard deviation of winning percentage of .098, rather than .100, and 22% of teams within ten games of first place, rather than 18%, which suggests that I must have excluded the Federal League teams from the original study. The actual standard deviation for 1950-1954 is .103, not .093, and I get 33% of the teams in that period within ten games of first, rather than 32%.

For the years 1970-1974, I get 25% of teams within ten games of first place, rather than 41%, which has to mean that when I did the original calculation I meant within ten games of first place in the *division*, rather than within ten games of the best team in the league. I'm not sure why I did it that way.

I probably studied five-year groups rather than complete decades because it was just so time-consuming to figure something like this at that time. You have to remember: there were no organized baseball databases at that time. In order to figure something like this, I had to type all of the data into a spreadsheet.

I will update these charts by including the last three decades, and, as that can now be done fairly easily, I will include the data for the entire decade, rather than a five-year sample:

Years	Standard Deviation of Won-Lost Percentage	Percentage of Teams Finishing Within Ten Games of First Place
1876-1879	.174	43%
1880-1889	.145	26%
1890-1899	.120	23%
1900-1909	.110	32%
1910-1919	.096	29%
1920-1929	.091	33%
1930-1939	.099	29%
1940-1949	.093	28%
1950-1959	.090	31%
1960-1969	.080	30%
1970-1979	.073	26%
1980-1989	.066	34%
1990-1999	.067	26%
2000-2009	.072	30%

The percentage of teams within ten games of first place in the years 1876-1879 is high because the schedule was very short...less than 70 games.

Essentially, what this data shows is that competitive balance—as measured by the standard deviation of team winning percentage—improved consistently from the beginnings of major league baseball until at least the 1980s. Since the 1980s, probably due to free agency, there has been *some* backward movement in competitive balance; however, the standard deviation of team winning percentage is still lower than it was in any decade prior to 1980.

———·—

ACKNOWLEDGEMENTS

———

Greg Pierce, for reading, selecting, and editing the articles herein.

Patricia Lynch, for designing the book. Tom Wright, for designing the cover.

John Dewan, who is the half-way point between Bill James and Greg Pierce.

Dave Studenmund, who guides and supervises Bill James On-line on a daily basis.

Andrew Yankech and Charles Fiore of ACTA Publications.

Jon Vrecsics of Baseball Info Solutions, who did his best to fact-check the book, although the author of course remains responsible for all mistakes, errors, and stupid statements within these covers.

Steve Moyer of Baseball Info Solutions.

Susan McCarthy, wife of the author.

To all others, named and unnamed, who have in any way contributed to the publication of this book…I thank you all.

———

WANT MORE BILL JAMES?

POPULAR CRIME
Reflections on the Celebration of Violence
by Bill James

James takes readers on an epic journey through the subject of popular crimes, from Lizzie Borden to the Lindbergh Baby, from the Black Dahlia to O.J. Simpson, from the Boston Strangler to JonBenet Ramsey—explaining how the crimes were committed, investigated, prosecuted, and chronicled and how they have profoundly influenced our culture.

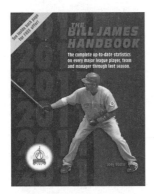

THE BILL JAMES HANDBOOK
by Bill James and the staff of Baseball Info Solutions

The first and best baseball annual each year, published and shipped by November 1 following the World Series. Contains all the lifetime stats of every active major league player that year, plus lots of cool leader boards, projections, articles, and the announcement of the annual Fielding Bible Awards.

HOW BILL JAMES CHANGED
OUR VIEW OF BASEBALL
By Colleagues, Critics, Competitors,
and Just Plain Fans
Edited by Gregory F. Augustine Pierce

Twelve original articles by John Dewan, Gary Huckabay, Susan McCarthy, Steve Moyer, Daryl Morey, Rob Neyer, Hal Richman, Alan Schwarz, Ron Shandler, Dave Studenmund, John Thorn, and Sam Walker, with a "Last Word" by Bill James and testimony by lots of fans whose lives were changed by reading his work.

Available from booksellers or ACTA Sports
www.actasports.com   800-397-2282